HABITS OF MIND
A Developmental Series

Assessing & Reporting on

HABITS OF MIND

Edited by
ARTHUR L. COSTA
and
BENA KALLICK

Foreword by David Perkins

Association for Supervision and Curriculum Development
Alexandria, Virginia USA

Association for Supervision and Curriculum Development
1703 N. Beauregard St. • Alexandria, VA 22311-1714 USA
Telephone: 1-800-933-2723 or 703-578-9600 • Fax: 703-575-5400
Web site: www.ascd.org • E-mail: member@ascd.org
Author guidelines: www.ascd.org/write

Printed in the United States of America.

ASCD Stock No. 100034   s8/00
ISBN-13: 978-0-87120-370-0   ISBN-10: 0-87120-370-7

Library of Congress Cataloging-in-Publication Data
Assessing and reporting on habits of mind / edited by Arthur L. Costa and Bena Kallick;
foreword by David Perkins.
     p. cm. — (Habits of mind ; bk. 3)
     Includes bibliographical references and index.
     "ASCD Stock No. 100034"—T.p. verso.
     ISBN 0-87120-370-7
     1. Thought and thinking—Study and teaching—United States. 2. Students—Rating of—United States.
I. Costa, Arthur L. II. Kallick, Bena. III. Title. IV. Series.

LB1590.3 .A77 2000
370.15'2—dc21

                                      00-010210

09 08 07 06 05   10 9 8 7 6 5 4 3

Native peoples teach that the ultimate norm for morality is the impact our choices have on persons living seven generations from now. If the results appear good for them, then our choices are moral ones; if not, they are immoral.

We therefore dedicate Habits of Mind: A Developmental Series to our children, our grandchildren, and their children's children.

HABITS OF MIND: A DEVELOPMENTAL SERIES

Habits of Mind Web site: http://www.habits-of-mind.net/

Habits of Mind Student Book Lists: available at http://www.ascd.org (search for "Habits of Mind: A Developmental Series"; a link to the book lists appears in the description)

ASSESSING AND REPORTING ON HABITS OF MIND

SERIES FOREWORD: THINKING ON THE ROAD OF LIFE

DAVID PERKINS

While driving into town a few years ago, I found myself behind a young man in a red convertible. Like many people, I have certain expectations about young men in red convertibles, but this young man surprised me. When we reached a railroad crossing, he was painfully careful. He slowed down as he approached the tracks. The closer he got to the tracks, the more he slowed. As his car passed over the tracks, it hardly was moving at all. At this point, with great care, the young man looked to the left, and then he looked to the right. No train was coming. Satisfied with his safety, he gunned the engine and sped off. The young man was careful—and yet he wasn't! Surely, the middle of the tracks isn't the best position from which to scan for oncoming trains!

This man's behavior provides a kind of a metaphor for the mission of the four-book series Habits of Mind: A Developmental Series. When on the road of life, we ought to be thoughtful about what we are doing. For example, we ought to manage impulsivity and strive for accuracy, two of the worthwhile habits of mind this series describes. Yet if good thinking is to help us out in life, it has to go on the road with us. The trouble is, good thinking often gets left behind altogether, or it's exercised in flawed ways that don't do the job, as this young man demonstrated.

How can we encourage ourselves and others—particularly students—to take good thinking on the road? Habits of Mind: A Developmental Series explores one answer to that challenge: the cultivation of habits of mind, or habits of thought as John Dewey (1933) called them. The idea is that we should have habits of mind such as persistence and flexible thinking, just as we have habits like brushing our teeth or putting the dog out or being kind to people. Habits are not behaviors we pick up and lay down whimsically or arbitrarily. They are behaviors we exhibit reliably on appropriate occasions, and they are smoothly triggered without painstaking attention.

The very notion of habits of mind, however, poses a conceptual puzzle. By definition, habits are routine, but good use of the mind is not. The phrase habits of mind makes for a kind of oxymoron, like "loud silence" or "safe risk." Indeed, the story of the young man in the convertible illustrates what can go wrong with cultivating habits of mind. Here you have a habit of mind (being careful) played out in a way that misses the point (the man looks for the train from the middle of the tracks!). The very automaticity of a habit can undermine its function. Habits like that don't serve us well on a literal highway—or on the metaphorical road of life, either.

Can one have a habit of mind that truly does its work? The resolution to this puzzle is not very difficult. There's a difference between the thinking required to manage a mental process and the thinking done by the process. A habitual mental process does not require a lot of management to launch and sustain it, but that process itself may conduct mindful thinking. It may involve careful examination of alternatives, assessment of risks and consequences, alertness to error, and so on. For example, I have a simple, well-entrenched habit for the road of life: looking carefully when I depart a setting to be sure that I'm not leaving anything behind. This habit triggers and runs off reliably, with very little need for mindful management. But the behaviors deployed by the habit are highly mindful: scrutinizing the setting, glancing under chairs for concealed objects, and peering into drawers and closets for overlooked items.

In all fairness, the man in the convertible displayed a habit with something of this quality, too. It was good that he looked both ways with care. No doubt his scan of the tracks was precise and sensitive. He certainly would have detected any oncoming train. The difficulty was that his habit included a bug, rather like a bug in a computer program. Although his habit had a thoughtful phase (scanning the tracks), he was not thoughtful about his habit (choosing the point where he should scan the tracks).

Thus, the idea of habits of mind is not self-contradictory. A behavior can be habitual in its management but mindful in what it does. Still, one might ask, "Why not have it all? Ideally, shouldn't thinking processes be mindfully managed, mindful through and through for that extra edge?" Probably not! At least three things are wrong with this intuitively appealing ideal.

First, having to manage a thinking process mindfully would likely reduce the thoughtfulness of the process itself. As Herbert Simon (1957) and many other psychologists have emphasized, we humans have a limited capacity for processing information. Committing the management of a thinking process to routine is one way to open up mental space for the work the process has to do. Second, life has many distractions and preoccupations. A well-developed habit is more likely to make its presence felt than a practice that always must be deployed with meticulous deliberateness.

The third objection to this ideal of thoroughly mindful thinking goes beyond these pragmatic considerations to a logical point. Suppose the general rule is that thinking processes need mindful management. Surely managing a thinking process is itself a thinking process, so that process, too, needs mindful management. And the process of managing needs mindful management, and so on. It is mindful management all the way up, an infinite tower of metacognition, each process managed by its own mindfully managed manager. Clearly this approach won't work. Enter habits of mind, an apt challenge to a misguided conception of thinking as thoroughly thoughtful.

The notion of habits of mind also challenges another conception: the notion of intelligence. Most of the research on human intelligence is emphatically "abilities centric" (Perkins, Jay, & Tishman, 1993; Perkins, 1995). As mentioned in Chapter 1 of Book 1, the IQ tradition sees intelligence as a pervasive, monolithic mental ability, summed up by IQ and Charles Spearman's (1904) "g" factor, a statistical construct representing general intelligence. A number of theorists have proposed that there are many kinds of mental ability (two to 150, according to one model developed by Guilford [1967]). Although this book is not a setting where these models bear review (see Perkins, 1995), most of these models have something in common: They treat intelligence as an "ability on demand." Intelligence becomes a matter of what you can do when you know what it is that you're supposed to try to do (such as complete this analogy, decide whether this inference is warranted, or find the best definition for this word).

Thinking in much of life is a different matter. In daily life, we not only have to solve problems, we also have to find them amid an ongoing, complex stream of stimuli imposing constant demands and distractions. On the road of life, our thinking is not just a matter of the thinking we can do when we know a peak performance is demanded. It also is a matter of our sensitivity to occasions and our inclination to invest ourselves in them thoughtfully. High mental ability alone may serve us well when we're sitting at a desk, our pencils poised, but good habits of mind keep us going in the rest of the world. This point is underscored by scholars such as philosopher Robert Ennis (1986), with his analysis of critical thinking dispositions; psychologist Jonathan Baron (1985), with his dispositional model of intelligence; and psychologist Ellen Langer (1989), with her conception of mindfulness.

A program of empirical research on thinking dispositions, which my colleague Shari Tishman and I have directed over the past several years, underscores what's at stake here (e.g., Perkins & Tishman, 1997). Working with students from middle to late elementary school, we investigated their performance on a variety of critical and creative thinking tasks involving narratives. Over and over again, we found that they could do far better than they did do when they explored options, considered pros and cons, and performed similar tasks. Their performance was limited because they often did not detect when such moves were called for. When they did detect what they should do, or when the places were pointed out, they easily could show the kind of thinking called for. They didn't lack intelligence in the sense of ability on demand, but they lacked the habits of mind that provide for ongoing alertness to shortfalls in thinking.

In that spirit, this series of four books speaks not just to intelligence in the laboratory but also to intelligent behavior in the real world. It addresses how we can help youngsters get ready for the road of life, a sort of "drivers' education" for the mind. Imagine what life would be like without good habits of various sorts. Our teeth would rot, our bodies collapse, our gardens wither, our tempers sour, and our friends drift away. We do better to the extent that we get direction from good habits, including habits of mind. When today's students hit the road, the ideas in Habits of Mind: A Developmental Series can help them ride on smooth mental wheels, checking for trains *before* they start over the tracks!

REFERENCES

Baron, J. (1985). *Rationality and intelligence*. New York: Cambridge University Press.

Dewey, J. (1933). *How we think: A restatement of the relation of reflective thinking to the education process*. New York: D. C. Heath.

Ennis, R. H. (1986). A taxonomy of critical thinking dispositions and abilities. In J. B. Baron & R. S. Sternberg (Eds.), *Teaching thinking skills: Theory and practice* (pp. 9–26). New York: W. H. Freeman.

Guilford, J. P. (1967). *The nature of human intelligence*. New York: McGraw-Hill.

Langer, E. J. (1989). *Mindfulness*. Reading, MA: Addison-Wesley.

Perkins, D. N. (1995). *Outsmarting IQ: The emerging science of learnable intelligence.* New York: The Free Press.

Perkins, D. N., Jay, E., & Tishman, S. (1993). Beyond abilities: A dispositional theory of thinking. *The Merrill-Palmer Quarterly, 39*(1), 1–21.

Perkins, D. N., & Tishman, S. (1997). *Dispositional aspects of intelligence.* Paper presented at the Second Spearman Seminar, The University of Plymouth, Devon, England.

Simon, H. A. (1957). *Models of man: Social and rational.* New York: Wiley.

Spearman, C. (1904). General intelligence, objectively defined and measured. *American Journal of Psychology, 15*, 201–209.

PREFACE TO THE SERIES

ARTHUR L. COSTA AND BENA KALLICK

Donna Norton Swindal, a resource teacher in Burnsville, Minnesota, recently shared an interesting story about a 4th grader who brought a newspaper clipping to class. The article described genocide in a troubled African country. After a lively discussion about what was happening there, one concerned classmate stated, "If those people would just learn to persist, they could solve their problems."

His philosophical colleague added, "If they would learn to listen with understanding and empathy, they wouldn't have this problem."

Yet another activist suggested, "We need to go over there and teach them the habits of mind!"

What are the "habits of mind" these concerned young citizens were so eager to share? They are the overarching theme of Habits of Mind: A Developmental Series, and they are the heart of the book you now hold in your hands.

THE BEGINNING

The ideas in Habits of Mind: A Developmental Series first started in 1982. Our beginning conversations about Intelligent Behaviors flourished into rich experiments with classroom practitioners until finally we arrived at this juncture: a series of four books to inspire the work of others. In our daily work with students and staff, we discovered that names were needed for the behaviors that would be expected from one another if, indeed, we were living in a productive learning organization. We came to call these dispositions "habits of mind," indicating that the behaviors require a discipline of the mind that is practiced so it becomes a habitual way of working toward more thoughtful, intelligent action.

The intent of Habits of Mind: A Developmental Series is to help educators teach toward these habits of mind, which we see as broad, enduring, and essential lifespan learnings that are as appropriate for adults as they are for students. Our hope is that by teaching students (and adults) the habits of mind, students will be more disposed to draw upon the habits when they are faced with uncertain or challenging situations. And, ultimately, we hope the habits will help educators develop thoughtful, compassionate, and cooperative human beings who can live productively in an increasingly chaotic, complex, and information-rich world (as the 4th graders above so aptly demonstrated!).

The most powerful communities use these habits of mind to guide all their work. Yet sometimes the practicality of school life requires that people make individual commitments with the hope that their beliefs and behaviors will affect the whole. Teaching with the habits of mind requires a shift toward a broader conception of educational outcomes and how they are cultivated, assessed, and communicated. Taken together, the four books in Habits of Mind: A Developmental Series aim to help you work toward and achieve these goals.

A DUAL PURPOSE

In this four-book series, we provide

- Descriptions and examples of the habits of mind.
- Instructional strategies intended to foster acquisition of these habits at school and at home.
- Assessment tools that provide a means of gathering evidence of student growth in the habits of mind.
- Ways of involving students, teachers, and parents in communicating progress toward acquiring the habits of mind.
- Descriptions from schools, teachers, and administrators about how they have incorporated the habits of mind and the effects of their work.

Our true intent for these books, however, is far more panoramic, pervasive, and long-range. Each book in the series works at two levels. The first level encompasses immediate and practical considerations that promote using the habits of mind in classrooms and schools every day. The second level addresses a larger, more elevated concern for creating a learning culture that considers habits of mind as central to building a thoughtful community. We summarize these levels as follows.

BOOK 1: *DISCOVERING AND EXPLORING HABITS OF MIND*

Level 1: Defining the habits of mind and understanding the significance of developing these habits as a part of lifelong learning.

Level 2: Encouraging schools and communities to elevate their level and broaden their scope of curricular outcomes by focusing on more essential, enduring lifespan learnings.

BOOK 2: *ACTIVATING AND ENGAGING HABITS OF MIND*

Level 1: Learning how to teach the habits directly and to reinforce them throughout the curriculum.

Level 2: Enhancing instructional decision making to employ content not as an end of instruction but as a vehicle for activating and engaging the mind.

BOOK 3: *ASSESSING AND REPORTING ON HABITS OF MIND*

Level 1: Learning about a range of techniques and strategies for gathering evidence of students' growth in and performance of the habits of mind.

Level 2: Using feedback to guide students to become self-assessing and to help school teams and parents use assessment data to cultivate a more thoughtful culture.

BOOK 4: *INTEGRATING AND SUSTAINING HABITS OF MIND*

Level 1: Learning strategies for extending the impact of habits of mind throughout the school community.

Level 2: Forging a common vision among all members of the educational community from kindergarten through post-graduate work: teachers, administrative teams, administrators, librarians, staff developers, teacher educators, school board members, and parents. This vision describes the characteristics of efficacious and creative thinkers and problem solvers.

In teaching for the habits of mind, we are interested in not only how many answers students know but also how students behave when they don't know an answer. We are interested in observing how students produce knowledge rather than how they merely reproduce it. A critical attribute of intelligent human beings is not only having information but also knowing how to act on it.

By definition, a problem is any stimulus, question, task, phenomenon, or discrepancy, the explanation for which is not immediately known. Intelligent behavior is performed in response to such questions and problems. Thus, we are interested in focusing on student performance under those challenging conditions—dichotomies, dilemmas, paradoxes, ambiguities and enigmas—that demand strategic reasoning, insightfulness, perseverance, creativity and craftsmanship to resolve them.

Teaching toward the habits of mind is a team effort. Because repeated opportunities over a long period are needed to acquire these habits of mind, the entire staff must dedicate itself to teaching toward, recognizing, reinforcing, discussing, reflecting on, and assessing the habits of mind. When students encounter these habits at each grade level in the elementary years and in each classroom throughout the secondary day—and when the habits also are reinforced and modeled at home—they become internalized, generalized, and habituated.

We need to find new ways of assessing and reporting growth in the habits of mind. We cannot measure process-oriented outcomes using old-fashioned, product-oriented assessment techniques. Gathering evidence of performance and growth in the habits of mind requires "kid watching." As students interact with real-life, day-to-day problems in school, at home, on the playground, alone, and with friends, teaching teams and other adults can collect anecdotes and examples of written and visual expressions that reveal students' increasingly voluntary and spontaneous use of these habits of mind. This work also takes time. The habits are never fully mastered, though they do become increasingly apparent over time and with repeated experiences and opportunities to practice and reflect on their performance.

Considered individually, each book helps you start down a path that will lead to enhanced curriculum, instruction, and assessment practices. Taken together, the books in Habits of Mind: A Developmental Series provide a road map for individuals, for classrooms, and ultimately for a full-system approach. For our purposes, we think a "system" is approached when the habits of mind are integrated throughout the culture of the organization. That is, when all individual members of a learning community share a common vision of the attributes of effective and creative problem solvers, when resources are allocated to the development of those dispositions; when strategies to enhance those characteristics in themselves and others are planned, and when members of the organization join in efforts to continuously assess, refine, and integrate those behaviors in their own and the organization's practices.

> *I can tell you right now that we will never be able to forget the habits of mind. They helped us so much! They taught us better*

ways of doing things and how to resolve problems! We learned respect and manners. My mother was so very impressed with this teaching. Also we learned that you need to get along with others and not to disrespect them either.

Excerpted from a 5th grader's
valedictorian address upon graduation from
Friendship Valley Elementary School, Westminster, Maryland

PREFACE TO BOOK 3

ARTHUR L. COSTA AND BENA KALLICK

What can educators look for to indicate that their students are progressing in their use of the habits of mind? Who needs to know about students' growth in the habits? And how should students' progress and growth be communicated? This is the stuff that Book 3, *Assessing and Reporting on Habits of Mind*, is made of.

Please note that throughout this book, we purposely avoid using the phrase "mastering the habits of mind." We believe no one ever fully masters the habits. We've not yet found the world's perfect listener or someone who persists in all endeavors or anyone who consistently manages personal impulsivity under high emotional stress. In assessing for and reporting about the habits of mind, we look for indicators of progress and growth, not some ultimate point of mastery.

Chapter 1 begins with descriptions of what educators and parents might hear students saying, or see them doing, as they improve their use of the habits of mind. This chapter addresses general indicators for each of the 16 habits. You will want to add to these lists to reflect the context and character of your students and school.

Chapter 2 invites staff members and students to dedicate themselves to enhanced learning through reflection. David Perkins (1995) believes that the capacity to learn from reflection is in itself a form of intelligence. Taking time to reflect may seem nearly impossible in our fast-paced, frenetic lives, but we offer many suggestions for helping students and staff members get into the habit of reflecting as a way of making greater meaning of their day-to-day experiences.

Because dispositions cannot be measured with product-oriented tools, Chapter 3 describes a variety of assessment techniques for the habits of mind. This chapter includes many practical examples from teachers and schools that have developed, tested, and refined these assessment tools. Chapter 3 also introduces the concept of the feedback spiral as a frame for observing and measuring continuous growth and learning.

Keep in mind that school staffs should share findings and systematically record indicators of growth over time. Such records provide feedback to staff, students, parents, school board members, and the community. Examining this accumulated information together encourages staff members to take pride in their accomplishments. Reflection can also highlight behaviors that need further cultivation, and it can ground decision making about allocating time and energy to refine assessment practices.

In Chapter 4, Steve Seidel demonstrates the power of reflective conversations. He describes a series of focused meetings where teachers looked at a single piece of student work for an extended time. The protocol they followed might serve as a springboard for similar rich reflections in your school or district.

Parents, staff members, and the community will find their perceptions about schooling transformed when they realize that the school's goals are to engage and enhance habits of mind rather than just convey traditional content. Chapter 5 contains suggestions for what to report, how to report it, and to whom information about the habits of mind should be reported.

The ultimate purpose of assessment is to guide students to become self-managing, self-monitoring, self-modifying, and self-assessing. We've missed the whole point of education if students graduate from school still dependent on others to tell them that their answers are right, their products are adequate, or their behavior is admirable. In Chapter 6, Steven Levy humorously—and pointedly—describes the patience and persistence required by a teacher intent on helping his students overcome their learned dependence on others.

In Chapter 7, Jodi Bongard and Judy Lemmel describe how they engaged parents in establishing a communication system that informs about students' progress in the habits of mind and also instructs in ways to support the habits at home.

We end Book 3 with a chapter on how to begin a schoolwide assessment program that guides students to be self-evaluative. Chapter 8 also describes ways to provide staff members with data to energize their curriculum and instructional decision making—and to support celebrations of their success!

REFERENCE

Perkins, D. (1995). *Outsmarting IQ: The emerging science of learnable intelligence.* New York: The Free Press.

From the Editors: Throughout the book, student names are fictitious.

1

Defining Indicators of Achievement

Arthur L. Costa and Bena Kallick

*How much do students really love to learn, to persist, to passionately attack
a problem or a task?*
. . . to watch some of their prized ideas explode and to start anew?
. . . to go beyond being merely dutiful or long-winded?
Let us assess such things.

Grant Wiggins

We are more likely to observe indicators of achievement if we first
take the time to specifically define those indicators. What kinds
of evidence show that students are acquiring the habits of mind?
This chapter contains general descriptions of indicators that show students
are acquiring, internalizing, and applying the habits of mind.

The habits of mind truly take on meaning when they are defined in the
context of day-to-day classroom life. Thus, teachers will want to consider
indicators for themselves first, then expand their consideration to include
students, colleagues, parents, and perhaps even other community members. The habits should be described in terms of the content being taught,
and they should be explained within the context of a particular classroom's
characteristics. Although the habits need to be considered within these
parameters, we suggest using the following general indicators as starting
points to decide what to look for when you use the feedback and assessment strategies described in Chapters 2 through 8.

PERSISTING

Be like a postage stamp: Stick to one thing until you get there.

Margaret Carty

Persistent students have systematic methods of analyzing a problem. They know how to begin, what steps must be performed, and what data need to be generated and collected. They also know when their theory or idea must be rejected so they can try another.

Students demonstrate growth in persistence when they increase their use of alternative problem-solving strategies. We see them collect evidence to indicate a problem-solving strategy is working. If the strategy isn't working, they back up and try another.

Students who have developed this habit of mind know how to draw upon a variety of resources. They ask others to clarify and to provide data. They consult books, dictionaries, and databases. Sometimes they go back to clarify a task or to analyze the directions.

Students who persist draw on previous experiences and apply that knowledge to solve the current problem. Thus, these students also demonstrate another habit of mind often linked to persistence: applying past knowledge to new situations. Many teachers find that several habits of mind naturally cluster together like this. As you consider indicators for a particular habit, you may also want to consider other habits linked to it.

MANAGING IMPULSIVITY

It is easier to suppress the first desire than to satisfy all that follow it.

Benjamin Franklin

As students become less impulsive, we observe them clarifying goals, planning a strategy for solving a problem, exploring alternative problem-solving strategies, and debating consequences of their actions before they begin. They consider before erasing, and they pay attention to their trial-and-error so they avoid making haphazard responses.

When students have developed the habit of managing impulsivity, they are engaged with problem solving, and they pay close attention to what is transpiring during a lesson or other classroom activity. They note what works as they solve a problem, and they redirect their strategies by developing a plan. They learn how to use "wait time" to their advantage. They also develop strategies for participating in activities, such as jotting down notes in a discussion so that they can remember the points they want to make when it's their turn to speak.

LISTENING WITH UNDERSTANDING AND EMPATHY

If there is any secret of success, it lies in the ability to get the other person's point of view and see things from his angle as well as from your own.
Henry Ford

We know students are improving their listening skills when they set aside their own value judgments, prejudices, and autobiographical stories to devote their mental energies to attending to another person. They demonstrate their understanding and empathy for another person's idea by paraphrasing it accurately, building upon it, clarifying it, or giving an example of it. We know students are listening to and internalizing others' ideas and feelings when we hear them say statements like these:

- "Peter's idea is . . . , but Sarah's idea is . . ."
- "Let's try Shelley's idea and see if it works."
- "Let me show you how Gina solved the problem, and then I'll show you how I solved it."

After paraphrasing another person's idea, a student may probe, clarify, or pose questions that extend the idea further: "I'm not sure I understand. Can you explain what you mean by . . . ?"

Empathy may be demonstrated by taking another's view or perspective: "I can see why Danielle views it that way. If I were her, I'd want the same." Empathy for another person's feelings or emotions is also demonstrated when the student labels those emotions or feelings:

- "You're *upset* because . . ."
- "You're *confused* about . . ."
- "You sure were *happy* about . . ."

THINKING FLEXIBLY

When one door is shut, another one opens.

Miguel de Cervantes

As students become more flexible in their thinking, we hear them considering, expressing, or paraphrasing other people's points of view or rationales. They state several ways of solving the same problem, and they evaluate the merits and consequences of two or more alternate courses of action. When making decisions, they often use words and phrases such as "however," "on the other hand," "if you look at it another way," or "John's idea is . . . , but Mary's idea is . . . ."

Students who have developed this habit of mind become systems thinkers. They analyze and scrutinize parts, but they also shift their perspective to the big picture, noting broader relationships, patterns, and interactions.

Students who are flexible thinkers generate many ideas. During a brainstorming session, their participation is usually fluent and productive. They are reluctant to see closure to group work. We hear them say, "Let's think of more ideas before we decide which one we want to use!"

THINKING ABOUT THINKING (METACOGNITION)

I thank the Lord for the brain He put in my head. Occasionally, I love to just stand to one side and watch how it works.

Richard Bolles

We can determine if students are becoming more aware of their own thinking when we give them the opportunity to describe what goes on in their heads as they think. Students who have found success with this habit can list the steps for how they will solve a problem, and they can tell you where they are in the sequence of those steps. They trace the pathways and blind alleys they took on the road to a problem's solution. They describe what data are lacking, and they also describe their plans for producing the missing data.

Students who have developed this habit are articulate about their reasoning processes. When asked to explain their answer to a problem, they give the solution and then describe the reasoning process that brought them to their conclusion. They also use proper cognitive terminology to describe their mental processes:

- "I have a *theory* that . . ."
- "I'm *conducting an experiment.*"
- "The *sequence of steps* in my *strategy* was first to . . . , and then I . . ."

STRIVING FOR ACCURACY

Measure a thousand times and cut once.

Turkish Proverb

As students mature in this habit of mind, we observe them taking greater care with their work. They check their projects, assignments, and tests again and again, asking others for feedback and correction. They establish standards of excellence, and they attempt to meet—and even exceed—those standards.

These students set higher and higher standards as they attempt to excel beyond a previous record. They express dissatisfaction with incomplete or sloppy work, and they request opportunities to improve upon their work. They also demonstrate a lack of complacency with the status quo.

QUESTIONING AND POSING PROBLEMS

The important thing is to not stop questioning.

Albert Einstein

Children pose questions naturally. They ask questions out of curiosity, intrigue, or interest. Yet with appropriate instruction—and time for reflection—children begin to ask questions more strategically. Trial lawyers use interrogation strategies with witnesses to build their cases. Scientists pose a series of questions to gather data to prove or disprove a theory. So, too, students begin to formulate questioning strategies and to link a sequence of questions to test hypotheses, guide data searches, clarify outcomes, or illuminate fallacious reasoning.

Maneuvering through the complexities of a task requires a conceptual framework from which questions can be formulated. Thus, strategic questioning implies that students hold a mental map in their head. For example, planning a trip requires questions about schedules, time lines, alternative destinations, arrivals, departures, and locations. Planning a science experiment requires similar kinds of questions about the task at hand: needed tools and supplies, possible strategies, the order of steps in the experiment, and evidence that the experiment has reached its conclusion.

Students' questions gain greater flair, power, and complexity with time and practice. They expand their range and repertoire of question types. Eventually, they can explain the function of a question and, when asked to explain their work, state the reason that they are asking a particular question.

Students soon see how the significance and power of good questioning can lead them to better understanding. Their class participation shows evidence of questions about the authority of a work, an author's point of view, the possible need for more data, or a provocative part to be examined. Their questions also stimulate others' thinking, raising even more classroom questions.

APPLYING PAST KNOWLEDGE TO NEW SITUATIONS

Learning is the ability to make sense out of something you observe based on your past experience and being able to take that observation and associate it with meaning.

Ruth and Art Winter

Students who have developed this habit of mind can abstract meaning from one experience and apply it to a new one. We know students are growing in this ability when we hear them make statements like, "This reminds me of . . . ," or "This is just like the time when we . . . !" We also see evidence of this ability when students explain what they are doing now with analogies about or references to previous experiences. We see them call upon their store of knowledge and experience to support theories that explain a situation or to outline a process to solve a new challenge.

We definitely know students are transferring their knowledge to new situations when parents and other teachers report how a student's thinking has changed at home or in other classes. For example, parents may report increased interest in school. They may see their child better plan the use of time and money. Or they may report increased organization of the child's room, books, and desk at home. At school, a social studies or industrial arts teacher may describe how a student used a problem-solving strategy that originally was learned in science or math class.

THINKING AND COMMUNICATING
WITH CLARITY AND PRECISION

A word to the wise is not sufficient if it doesn't make sense.

James Thurber

As students acquire more exact language for describing their work, they begin to recognize concepts, identify key attributes, distinguish similarities and differences, and make more thorough and rational decisions. If value judgments are made, students spontaneously offer the criteria on which the judgments were based. When comparing, they describe the attributes and significance of their comparisons. They state the reasons behind their generalizations, and they provide data to support their conclusions.

Students who have developed this habit use the correct names for objects, ideas, and processes. When universal labels are unavailable, they use analogies such as "that's crescent shaped" or "it's like a bow tie." They speak in complete sentences, voluntarily provide supporting evidence for their ideas, elaborate, clarify, and define their terminology. Overall, their speech becomes more concise, descriptive, and coherent.

GATHERING DATA THROUGH ALL SENSES

It is not easy to describe the sea without the mouth.

Kokyu

Students who have developed this habit feel free to engage and explore all their senses. When they are confronted with a problem, they suggest strategies for gathering data or for solving the problem that incorporate a variety of senses: visualizing, building a model, feeling textures, acting out or dancing a poem or prose, listening to and visualizing recurring cycles and patterns, or moving to the rhythms. They seek ways to engage all the senses, wanting to hold, touch, feel, taste, smell, and experience objects and events.

These students' enriched written and oral language displays an ever-increasing range of sensory metaphors: kinesthetic, auditory, visual, gustatory, and olfactory. They experiment with vivid, sensuous, and evocative descriptions and alliterations, describing "a waterfall of problems," "atonal music slapping my ears," or "gardenias: The gods' belief in aromatherapy."

CREATING, IMAGINING, INNOVATING

Originality is simply a pair of fresh eyes.

Thomas Wentworth Higginson

We know students are creating, imagining, and innovating when we see them deliberately and voluntarily employ strategies for stimulating, generating, and releasing inventive ideas for a new task. They expand the possibility of creative insight by preparing their minds with much knowledge about a subject. Then, they generate options and possibilities.

When students who have developed this habit face an impasse, they deliberately widen the scope of their search with techniques such as brainstorming, mind mapping, synectics, or metaphorical thinking. They search for theories, explanations, and frameworks that have generative potentials, which lead to further meanings. They pursue promising theories, and they constantly hunt for "nubs" and "kernels" of viable ideas. They explore options, think of possibilities, generate strategies, and explore consequences (Perkins, 1995).

RESPONDING WITH WONDERMENT AND AWE

The real mark of the creative person is that the unforeseen problem is a joy and not a curse.

Norman H. Mackworth

Students who respond with wonderment and awe display an "I can" and "I enjoy" attitude. These students seek out problems to solve for themselves and to submit to others. They make up problems to solve on their own, and they request them from others. These students solve problems with increasing independence, without the teacher's help or intervention. We hear their growing autonomy in statements such as, "Don't tell me the answer! I can figure it out by myself!"

Students who have developed this habit are curious, and they derive pleasure from thinking. Their environment attracts their inquiry as their senses capture the rhythm, patterns, shapes, colors, and harmonies around them. They will stand transfixed in the beauty of a sunset, study with fascination the geometrics of a spider web, or be charmed by the opening of a spring bud. They can't help but exclaim their exuberance: "Wow!" "Cool!" "Awesome!" "All right!"

Students who have developed this habit also display compassionate behavior toward other life forms. These students understand the need to protect the environment. They respect the roles and values of other human beings, and they perceive the delicate worth, uniqueness, and relationships of everything and everyone they encounter.

TAKING RESPONSIBLE RISKS

There are risks and costs to action. But they are far less than the long-range risks of comfortable inaction.

John F. Kennedy

Although students learn to manage their impulsivity, at the same time they also begin to show evidence of taking more risks in their work. Maybe they write dialogue for the first time in their stories. Perhaps they use humor to make a particular point, or they throw out an idea in a discussion without qualifying it by saying, "I might be wrong about this . . . ," or "I know this may not be what is called for, but . . ."

Students who are practicing responsible risk taking show a willingness to try out new strategies, techniques, and ideas. They explore new art media, wanting to experiment with different effects. They are willing to test a new hypothesis, even when they feel skeptical. In a group, they often can be heard saying, "Let's try it!" or "What's the worst thing that can happen if we try? We'll only be wrong!"

FINDING HUMOR

I'd rather be a failure at something I enjoy than be a success at something I hate.

George Burns

As students develop this habit, they learn to distinguish between clowning around and using humor to increase their own or a group's productivity. They learn not to take themselves too seriously. They joke about errors they have made, poke fun at themselves, and seek the humor and absurdity in situations that seem to warrant it.

Students who have developed this habit are often observed using humor to relieve a group's tension. They know the difference between using humor antagonistically and using humor to raise their own and others' spirits. They generate stories, metaphors, and puns. They are also quick to laugh and collect humorous stories to relate to others.

THINKING INTERDEPENDENTLY

Community is . . . a dynamic set of relationships in which a synergistic, self-regulating whole is created out of the combination of individual parts into a cohesive, identifiable, unified form.

Center for the Study of Community
Santa Fe, New Mexico

Students who think interdependently set aside their own ego needs to serve others. They devote their energies to enhancing the group's resourcefulness. They put others before themselves, and they derive satisfaction when others excel and are recognized.

As work increases in abstraction and complexity, we are pressed to find its meaning through what Vygotsky calls "social construction" of knowledge. Students show evidence of increased interdependence in group work and discussions when they focus on analysis, synthesis, and evaluation. Their language reflects their desire to understand how others are thinking and to keep making sense out of the problem or text. They offer interpretations and hypotheses to the group, and at the same time, they build on other people's ideas. They often can be heard saying, "When I see this, it makes me think this is what is happening. What do you think?"

Students showing evidence of this habit monitor the equality of group participation. They show concern for all members of the group, and they are aware of classmates who are isolated or excluded from the work. We hear them say, "We haven't heard from Rick yet" or "Tess hasn't had a chance to speak." They help each other learn to ensure that all members of the group contribute to the task and succeed. Students demonstrating this habit not only contribute to but learn from the group: "You really helped me see . . . ," or "Thanks for showing me how to . . ."

REMAINING OPEN TO CONTINUOUS LEARNING

The value of the average conversation could be enormously improved by the constant use of four simple words: "I do not know."

Andre Maurois

Although it is human to defend our biases, beliefs, actions, and knowledge, it is also human to transcend the protective instinct by tapping into the courage to learn and change. For students who have developed this habit, the encounters, events, and circumstances of life in school and community become invitations to improve themselves by remaining open to continuous learning. As Ethyl Barrymore observed, "It's what you learn after you know it all that counts."

Students who have developed this habit of mind use feedback. They always assume that there is more to learn. We see them ask the next set of questions after a conclusion, ask for peer feedback, and seek new resources to modify their knowledge. They realize that to get anywhere always implies a further journey to the next place. They understand that expertise is not knowing everything but knowing the next, more sophisticated level of the work. As each level of knowledge is achieved, a whole new set of questions emerges.

These students are willing to let go of the need for the safety of "rightness" to claim the uncertainty of new investigations and knowledge. They strive to learn and are dissatisfied with mere judgments. They demonstrate a willingness to risk the potential of a lesser grade for the possibility of a greater challenge. They are resourceful, and they use the resourcefulness of others. They are proud to admit that they don't know an answer or solution, and they are intrigued by the potential for further inquiry. We hear them say things like, "That's an interesting idea. How could we find out more about it?"

*   *   *

There is great value in making the habits of mind explicit with indicators that guide us in observing growth and improvement. As we develop a common language for describing the habits of mind, we bring ourselves to a highly personal understanding of their power, and we realize the power each of us, as individuals, can bring to groups as we intentionally employ the habits. Assessment requires definition, which in turn serves as a cognitive map for behavior. And regularly changing behaviors creates the habit.

REFERENCE

Perkins, D. (1995). Insight in minds and genes. In J. J. Sternberg & J. E. Davidson (Eds.), *The nature of insight* (pp. 495–533). Cambridge, MA: The MIT Press.

2

LEARNING THROUGH REFLECTION

ARTHUR L. COSTA AND BENA KALLICK

A defining condition of being human is that we have to understand the meaning of our experience.

Jack Mezirow

Most of us go through life viewing our experiences as isolated, unrelated events. We also view these happenings simply as the experiences they are, not as opportunities for learning. Psychologists refer to this type of life-view as an "episodic grasp of reality" (Feuerstein, Rand, Hoffman, & Miller, 1980), and it is not a habit we want to pass along to children. Instead, we want students to get into the habit of linking and constructing meaning from their experiences. Such work requires reflection.

Reflection has many facets. For example, reflecting on work enhances its meaning. Reflecting on experiences encourages insight and complex learning. We foster our own growth when we control our learning, so some reflection is best done alone. Reflection is also enhanced, however, when we ponder our learning with others.

Reflection involves linking a current experience to previous learnings (called scaffolding). Reflection also involves drawing forth cognitive and emotional information from several sources: visual, auditory, kinesthetic, and tactile. To reflect, we must act upon and process the information, synthesizing and evaluating the data. In the end, reflecting also means applying what we've learned to contexts beyond the original situations in which we learned something.

Valuing Reflection

The art of teaching is the art of assisting discovery.

Mark Van Doren

Teachers who promote reflective classrooms ensure that students are fully engaged in the process of making meaning. They organize instruction so that students are the producers, not just the consumers, of knowledge. To best guide children in the habits of reflection, these teachers approach their role as a "facilitator of meaning making."

In the role of facilitator, the teacher acts as an intermediary between the learner and the learning, guiding each student to approach the learning activity in a strategic way. The teacher helps each student monitor individual progress, construct meaning from the content learned *and* from the process of learning it, and apply the learnings to other contexts and settings. Learning becomes a continual process of engaging the mind that transforms the mind.

Unfortunately, educators don't often ask students to reflect on their learning. Thus, when students *are* asked to reflect on an assignment, they are caught in a dilemma: "What am I supposed to do? How do I 'reflect'? I've already completed this assignment! Why do I have to think about it anymore?"

Students who are inexperienced with reflection offer simple answers such as, "This was an easy assignment!" or "I really enjoyed doing this assignment." If we want students to get in the habit of reflecting deeply on their work—and if we want them to use habits of mind such as applying past knowledge to new situations, thinking about thinking (metacognition), and remaining open to continuous learning—we must teach them strategies to derive rich meaning from their experiences.

Setting the Tone for Reflection

Most classrooms can be categorized in one of two ways: active and a bit noisy, with students engaged in hands-on work; or teacher oriented, with students paying attention to a presentation or quietly working on individual tasks. Each of these teaching environments sets a tone and expectation. For example, when students work actively in groups, we ask them to use their "six-inch" voices. When we ask them to attend to the teacher, we also request that they turn their "eyes front." When they work individually at their desks, we ask them not to bother other learners.

Teachers must signal a shift in tone when they ask students to reflect on their learning. Reflective teachers help students understand that the students will now look back rather than move forward. They will take a break from what they have been doing, step away from their work, and ask themselves, "What have I (or we) learned from doing this activity?" Some teachers use music to signal the change in thinking. Others ask for silent thinking before students write about a lesson, assignment, or other classroom task.

In the reflective classroom, teachers invite students to make meaning from their experiences overtly in written and oral form. They take the time to invite students to reflect on their learnings, to compare intended with actual outcomes, to evaluate their metacognitive strategies, to analyze and draw causal relationships, and to synthesize meanings and apply their learnings to new and novel situations. Students know they will not "fail" or make a "mistake," as those terms are generally defined. Instead, reflective students know they can produce personal insight and learn from *all* their experiences.

GUIDING STUDENT REFLECTION

To be reflective means to mentally wander through where you have been and to try to make some sense out of it. Most classrooms are oriented more to the present and the future than they are to the past. Such orientation means that students (and teachers) find it easier to discard what has happened and to move on without taking stock of the seemingly isolated experiences of the past.

Teachers use many strategies to guide students through a period of reflection. We offer several here: discussions, interviews, questioning, and logs and journals.

DISCUSSIONS

Sometimes, encouraging reflection is as simple as inviting students to think about their thinking. Students realize meaning making is an important goal when reflection becomes the topic of discussion. For example, conduct discussions about students' problem-solving processes. Invite students to share their metacognition, reveal their intentions, detail their strategies for solving a problem, describe their mental maps for monitoring their problem-solving process, and reflect on the strategy to determine its adequacy. During these kinds of rich discussions, students learn how to listen to and explore the implications of each other's metacognitive strategies. The kind of listening required during such discussions also builds habits of mind related to empathy, flexibility, and persistence.

INTERVIEWS

Interviews are another way to lead students to share reflections about their learning and their growth in the habits of mind. A teacher can interview a student, or students can interview classmates. Set aside time at the end of a learning sequence—a lesson, a unit, a school day, or a school year—to question each other about what has been learned. Guide students to look for ways they can apply their learnings to future settings. Interviews also provide teachers and students with opportunities to model and practice a variety of habits: listening with understanding and empathy, thinking and communicating with clarity and precision, and questioning and posing problems.

QUESTIONING

A classroom atmosphere grounded in trust—and supported by well-designed questions—will invite students to reveal their insights, understandings, and applications of their learnings and the habits of mind. You might pose questions such as these with each student:

• As you reflect on this semester's work, which of the habits of mind were you most aware of in your own learnings?
• What metacognitive strategies did you use to monitor your performance of the habits of mind?
• Which habit of mind will you focus your energies on as you begin our next project?
• What insights have you gained as a result of employing these habits of mind?
• As you think about your future, how might these habits of mind be used as a guide in your life?

LOGS AND JOURNALS

Logs and journals are another tool for student reflection. Periodically ask students to reread their journals, comparing what they knew at the beginning of a learning sequence with what they know now. Ask them to select significant learnings, envision how they could apply these learnings to future situations, and commit to an action plan to consciously modify their behaviors. (See also the section on "Journals and Logs" in Chapter 3.)

MODELING REFLECTION

Students need to encounter reflective role models. Many teachers find such models in novels where the characters take a reflective stance as they consider their actions. A variety of novels and films use the design element of reflection as the way to tell a story. For example, in Marcel Proust's *Swann's Way*, the main character is affected by the smell of a "petit Madeleine" that reminds him of his past. Proust uses this device to dig into the character's past. In Mem Fox's *Wilfrid Gordon McDonald Partridge*, Wilfrid discovers that life's meaning can come from the retrieval of powerful memories. The memories truly are given meaning, however, through making them explicit to someone else.

Although fictional role modeling is useful, students also need to see adults—parents, teachers, and administrators—reflect on their practice. Perhaps you can offer an example from your own work. We offer here an excerpt from Bena Kallick's journal reflecting on a workshop session. She sent her reflection to the workshop participants. Here's the excerpt:

> To: The third-year teachers and mentors
> From: Bena Kallick
> Re: Yesterday's session
>
> Reflecting on the day, I am still mad at myself for not listening more closely to your needs for the afternoon session. I wanted to share some of my thoughts with you.
>
> First, I find that I can use the habits of mind as one lens for reflection. As I reconsidered yesterday, there were four habits that I focused on: listening with understanding and empathy, thinking flexibly, managing impulsivity, and remaining open to continuous learning.
>
> *Listening with understanding and empathy.* One of the strengths in my work is my capacity to stay immersed in the work of others. I need to be able to listen to the surface text of the work, pay attention to the subtext of the individual (the context of the classroom, the personality of the teacher, the intentions and values that are expressed as the person presents the work), and make certain that my comments and critique are

in tune with the person who I hope will be able to make use of them. I felt that our group was tuned to the work that was presented and that I was able to model that level of listening. As a result, I think that the presenters were able to listen to their own work more deeply.

The other half of my listening, however, was not as attuned. Patricia tried to suggest that we make time for you to share your own work in the afternoon, but because I lunched with Michelle and was involved with some of the issues and problems she was working on, I lost some of my perspective on where the group was. As a result, I jumped in with the plan to look at the possibility for "brand x" rubrics. Although I cast the afternoon for the possibility of your working on your own rubrics, I observed that almost everyone either worked on the general rubric (with energy and commitment) or started to do their own work for the classroom. I thought that most people were using the time productively, and so I did not listen carefully to Patricia's concerns. I should have lunched with Patricia and David, talked through what was in my head for the afternoon, and listened at that time for their read of the group and its needs.

Thinking flexibly. I always pride myself on the degree to which I am willing to shift plans and respond to the group's immediate needs. That strength, however, can also become a weakness—and I think that happened yesterday. When Dan suggested that we move to developing outcomes that would work across the disciplines, I immediately went there without checking with the group. Maybe that happened because the question is of intellectual interest to me right now and I also wanted to work on it. I have been struggling with how to develop a rubric that would be sufficiently rigorous and, at the same time, descriptive enough to provide a set of criteria for students that would show them what was expected regardless of subject. Clear criteria would address a question such as, "Why do we need to write properly if I am in a science class?" To me, these criteria are a significant part of building a learning culture. I was exploring using the criteria in relation to the habits of mind—I will develop this thought more fully in a moment.

Managing impulsivity. Well, this is where the habits intersect and sometimes feel contradictory. I moved very quickly with Dan's suggestion. I would say that I did not manage my impulsivity. Can you be both flexible and manage your impulsivity at the same time? I think the way to do that is to check your moves. I should have done so with the group instead of assuming I knew where to go. Had I managed my impulsive act through a quick check on the afternoon agenda, we might have gone down the same path, or a different one, and at least made the decision together.

Remaining open to continuous learning. I started thinking about Evonne Goolagong. (She's a really great tennis player. What I always admired about her was her grace, agility, and enormous flexibility. She had all the strokes, and often what got in her way of winning was that she did not make the right choice of stroke for the occasion.) I think I am at a point in my career where I have many choices in my repertoire for each teaching situation. Sometimes I do not take the time to think through which is the right choice for the occasion. I am finding it easy to excuse impulsive behavior by thinking of it as flexible behavior. Because I am an "in the moment" teacher, I need to pay attention to this more than I have been recently. I am grateful to you yesterday for reminding me of the importance of this dynamic in order for me to continue to be the teacher I imagine I would like to be!

After this particular reflection, Kallick worked with the teachers to design their next session to better meet everyone's needs. Sharing parts of the reflection brought them to another level of understanding as they worked together in a learning community. Reflection can bring the same spirit of community to your classroom, too.

Students also learn much when they see examples of reflection from other students' journals. You might want to cull a variety of examples to share. Here is a reflection from a group journal written by students from the Communications Academy at Sir Francis Drake High School in San Anselmo, California:

Today our group spent most of the time reading articles and the ballot info pamphlet. We have all participated and have been open and informative. Our goal seems to be execution of the actual set criteria for our project. . . .

We are passing around our wonderful journal to write down what we want to do or improve on for ourselves. I want to work on reading. I find myself reading enough to slide by but not enough to be fully educated in the subject. It takes a lot of time, so I need to find some of that, too. I want to be able to answer the questions I have asked with precision and accuracy. My stretch goal would be to do everything assigned to me completed and on time. If I start to slack off, just kick me back into place. . . .

I want to be more patient. I also feel I talk a lot and don't mean to. I want to try to listen with understanding and empathy.

The students at University Heights School in New York City are required to reflect on the habits of mind they have adopted when they present their portfolios to a panel of judges. The following excerpt is a reflection from one student:

> Through "Thinking Critically and Questioning," we investigate questions, myths, and even proven knowledge. From that we gain intelligence (learning from proof, not opinion) and experiences to find what we believe to be the truth. . . .
>
> I learned the importance of an education. Ignorance is a weakness. It fogs the mind and blurs the human eye. Only knowledge can clear our visions of this weakening lack of thought. . . .
>
> I learned the value of our pride. In my opinion, those who were forced to serve without pay were not slaves. They were captives to slaves of greed.
>
> Now that I have this strengthened knowledge, I must apply it to my life. But the success of that assignment can only be judged by me. Only I know what is happiness and beauty in this mind and it will take me an entire lifetime to apply what I have learned to my existence.

DEVELOPMENTAL ISSUES

The work of educators at Croton Elementary School in Croton-on-Hudson, New York, shows how the quality of students' reflections changes as children develop their reading and writing skills. When kindergartners were asked to reflect orally, they gave rich descriptions of their work. But as they developed their writing ability and were encouraged to write their own reflections, the reflections became less descriptive. This change puzzled the teachers until they realized that students are more concerned about spelling, punctuation, and other aspects of editing when they first learn to write. Because students do not have a great deal of fluency with their writing, they are more limited in what they describe.

In contrast, when meeting with the teacher, the kindergartners elaborated on what they wrote about their work. And once students became more fluent with their writing skills, they were able to represent their reflective thoughts more easily.

TEACHING STUDENTS HOW TO REFLECT

Initially, students often offered stereotypical comments such as, "This was fun!" or "I chose this piece of work because it is my best." Teachers realized that they needed to spend time teaching students how to reflect. They asked students, "What does a reflection look like when it really tells you something about the experience?" After considerable discussion—and after considering models of reflection from students and published authors—the students began to understand what was called for. Reflection was not a time for testimonials about how good or bad the experience was. Instead, reflection was the time to consider what was learned from the experience. Reflection was a time to describe what students saw in their own work that changed, needed to change, or might need to be described so another person might understand its meaning.

Figure 2.1 (see p. 24) shows how teachers characterized student work as students acquired the capacity for reflection. The teachers then summarized key statements that students made about their work when asked the question, "What would I change to make my work better?" Students from kindergarten through 2nd grade made comments such as these:

- I would add to the picture.
- I would use what I know to show more in the picture.
- I would add what is missing.
- I would be more careful.

Students in 3rd and 4th grade made comments like these:

- I would correct.
- I would proofread.
- I would pay attention to conventions.
- I would extend more.
- I would stay to the subject.

Teachers used these phrases to describe 3rd and 4th grade students' writing as the teachers reflected upon it:

- Uses humor.
- Talks about genre or type of writing.
- Attends to style (uses dialogue).
- Describes well enough for a reader to picture what was written.

FIGURE 2.1
Students' Stages of Reflection

Kindergarten

Describes what is drawn.

Focuses on drawing.

Comments on realism.

Shows interest (what student really loves).

Mentions use of color.

Mentions use of letters.

Pays attention to what letters spell.

1st Grade

Focuses on conventions.

Wants papers to have a neat appearance.

Talks about what was liked in drawing.

2nd Grade

Focuses on details.

Focuses on colors.

Shows development of an idea.

Relates to content of story (how student feels about the content of what was written).

3rd–5th Grade (Learning-to-Read Stage)

Responds in depth to dictation.

Starts to write by self.

- Focuses on script.
- Focuses on description.
- Offers information.
- Is interesting.
- Works hard.
- Is exciting.
- Attends to the reader.
- Is clear.
- Does not drag writing out.
- Uses descriptive words.

Through this experience, the teachers realized that the questions they asked might limit students' responses. They reminded themselves that the purpose of reflection is threefold:

• To help students become more aware of their writing: what makes writing work and what does not.

• To help students take more responsibility for their writing: to know that writing must be understood by an audience and to learn how to anticipate a reader's response through self-evaluation.

• To see growth in writing over the school year and to be able to talk about that growth with students' parents.

Teachers emphasized to students that the purpose of reflection was not to develop a carefully crafted piece of writing, but to develop the capacity for metacognition.

SENTENCE STEMS

Sentence stems can stimulate reflections. Use them in conferences (where reflection can be modeled), or put them on a sheet for students who choose writing to jump-start their reflections. Here are examples of possible sentence stems:

• I selected this piece of writing because . . .
• What really surprised me about this piece of writing was . . .
• When I look at my other pieces of writing, this piece is different because . . .
• What makes this piece of writing strong is my use of . . .
• Here is one example from my writing to show you what I mean.
• What I want to really work on to make my writing better for a reader is . . .

STUDENT CHOICES

Students may prefer simply to describe what is going on in the writing in their own way. When students set their goals, they will use their reflections as a basis for directing their learning journey. Students might collect work throughout the year as part of a portfolio process. Every quarter they can review the work in their collection folders and choose one or two pieces to enter into their portfolio. When they make those choices, they can take the opportunity to reflect on the reasons for their choices and to set goals for their next quarter's work.

BUILDING THE VOICES OF REFLECTION

The ultimate intent of teaching reflection is to get students into the habit of reflecting on their own actions and constructing meaning from those experiences. When they develop the habits of mind related to reflection, they will hear both an internal and an external voice of reflection.

INTERNAL VOICE

The internal voice of reflection is self-knowledge. Self-knowledge is difficult to detail, but we can define self-knowledge as both *what* and *how* you are thinking. Self-knowledge includes ways of thinking that may not be visible to you consciously. Given our culture, students have difficulty realizing that they need to engage in "self-talk." Here are suggestions for helping students develop the internal voice of reflection. Ask students to

• Write a letter to themselves detailing what they learned from an experience.
• Send themselves a letter of advice, reminding themselves of what to look out for the next time they do something.
• Interview themselves.
• Make a list of connections they see between their work and others' work. Include peers' work along with work that has been studied in the classroom.
• Record the steps they go through to solve a problem. Guide them to comment on how useful those steps were.

EXTERNAL VOICE

Students hear an external voice of reflection in others' comments, suggestions, assessments, evaluations, and feedback. External sharing of reflections is important because this kind of reflection multiplies the learning for each individual. As students review the learning events that have taken place, they give their learning new meaning. The opportunity to share often validates a student's internal conversation. Here are suggestions for helping students develop the capacity for sharing their reflections:

• Sit in a circle. Ask each person to share one reflection on the day's activities.
• Organize small-group reflections in which students share their thoughts. Then ask a reporter to present those thoughts to the whole class.
• Invite students to share problem-solving strategies. Ask them to focus

on how many different ways they can effectively solve a problem.

• Ask students to share at least one example in which they observed their group using the habits of mind.

During these classroom experiences, teachers have an opportunity to model the habits of mind themselves. They can show evidence of good listening skills, probe for clarity and understanding, ask thoughtful questions, and share metacognitive thinking. Through experience and continuous modeling, the class begins to learn how to use the habits of mind in reflective conversations, which strengthens the transfer to the internal voice of reflection.

DOCUMENTING REFLECTIONS

Many teachers document reflective conversations as a way of assessing progress with the habits of mind. For example, some teachers create a notebook tabbed with each student's name. They also keep sticky labels close at hand. When a student makes a significant comment that shows evidence of using a habit of mind, the teacher jots down the key words from the comment on a label and sticks the label on the tabbed page for that student. This record provides a rich source of information for a conference or student report.

You might also consider reading student journals and noting how student reflections are developing. Keep a record for each student with notes about whether the student has moved from superficial to in-depth reflections. Some indicators of in-depth reflections are making specific reference to the learning event, providing examples and elaboration, making connections to other learning, and discussing modifications based on insights from this experience.

Developing the habits of mind related to continuous growth and improvement requires the capacity to be self-reflective. As students reflect on their learning, they gain important assessment information about how they perceive the efficacy of their thinking.

*   *   *

Many of us grow up thinking of mistakes as bad, viewing errors as evidence of fundamental incapacity. This negative thinking pattern can create a self-fulfilling prophecy, which undermines the learning process.

To maximize our learning it is essential to ask: "How can we get the most from every mistake we make?"

Michael Gelb and Tony Buzan

REFERENCE

Feuerstein, R., Rand, Y., Hoffman, M., & Miller, R. (1980). *Instrumental enrichment: An intervention program for cognitive modifiability.* Baltimore, MD: University Park Press.

3

Assessing the Habits of Mind

Arthur L. Costa and Bena Kallick

What gets measured gets done. Measurement is the heart of any improvement process. It must begin at the outset of the program, be visible, and done by the natural work group itself.

Tom Peters

When educators are serious about helping students develop the habits of mind, they find ways to make those habits integral to both assessment *and* feedback. Keep in mind the distinction between those two aspects of evaluation. Assessment without feedback merely serves as judgment. Feedback is the part of assessment that enables us to make sense of judgment and improve our work. Educators must consciously create school cultures that require both feedback and assessment. This chapter considers different ways to achieve this goal.

GUIDING ASSUMPTIONS

The following assumptions support a feedback and assessment system that promotes students' use of the habits of mind:

- Data energize learning.
- Students must set and meet goals.
- Schools must become learning organizations.
- Assessment requires self-regulation.

Data Energize Learning

Students learn and grow when they have the opportunity to consider external and internal data. External data include feedback from teacher evaluations and test results. They also include "coaching" information from peers and teachers.

Many students are familiar with various types of external data, but they are less conversant with internal data. The term "internal data" describes information gained from personal reflection. Students need opportunities to self-evaluate and generate these kinds of data. They must learn how to compare their current performance to previous performance, and they must learn how to analyze their performance in terms of benchmarks for "good" performance.

Remember that neither external nor internal data are useful for learning unless feedback is frequent and stated in constructive terms. Feedback given too long after an assessment or learning event won't influence a student in the same way as data offered almost immediately. Also, students find it more helpful to hear constructive comments on their work. They need (and want!) to hear what they can do, not just what they cannot do.

Students Must Set and Meet Goals

Students need to participate in the goal-setting process. It has always seemed a puzzle that students are expected to reach goals that others have set for them. Michael Jordan, an extraordinary athlete, states, "You have to expect things of yourself before you can do them." The key to a self-directed and self-modifying learner is the ability to set meaningful goals and find ways of knowing whether those goals have been met and to what standard. Students must participate in the goal-setting process and create the work plans that will help them fulfill the requirements of the stated goals.

As part of the process, students and teachers should agree on documentation methods so that students are not only aware of their goals but can also monitor and celebrate their successes. As they monitor their goals, they can modify their strategies if they are not moving toward success.

Schools Must Become Learning Organizations

At first glance, this assumption seems somewhat obvious, but the thought behind it bears restating: Schools must become the kinds of learning organizations where every participant is continuously growing and learning. Assessment won't be valued unless it is a part of every person's work in the organization.

Such integration means that when data energize learning, teachers will use data as catalysts for learning about students, students will use data as sources for improving their work, and boards of education will use data to create opportunities for staff professional development. When we expect students to participate in setting and meeting goals, we consider all of us as students of teaching and learning. Every member of a school community recognizes the significance of setting goals that benchmark growth and learning. And every member learns how to celebrate the successes that lead the organization to greater learning and improvement.

ASSESSMENT REQUIRES SELF-REGULATION

All programs—and the individuals working in them—must become self-managing, self-monitoring, and self-modifying. This process of assessment and feedback ultimately leads to learners who are self-assessing. Self-knowledge is the first step in this kind of self-assessment.

Much of the work of self-evaluation is developed through metacognitive processes. Students need to be able to answer questions such as these:

- What is the best environment for your learning?
- Where do you choose to study?
- Where do you choose to work creatively?
- How do you work with others?
- What is your preferred learning mode (e.g., visual or kinesthetic)?
- What do you consider are your talents or strengths (e.g., arts, oral presentations, persuasive arguments)?
- Where do your interests lie?
- How do you use criteria to determine whether your work is good?
- Do you check for accuracy and precision?
- Are you persistent as you develop your work?

Many teachers ask students to reflect on questions such as these regularly. The self-assessment data generated by these questions promote students' learning and growth. The data also provide useful information for teachers as they facilitate learning.

Self-knowledge builds on internal and external reflections and observations. Feedback from teachers is a rich source of external data. Teachers can give evaluative feedback about thinking by focusing on a variety of questions:

- What is the student's disposition or attitude toward learning?

• How does the student think about assessing information?
• What information does the student consider important?
• How does the student use a reasoning process to think about the information being gathered?
• How does the student use strategies to solve problems?
• How does the student communicate the results of the student's learning?
• What is evidenced in the student's performance as the student applies this learning to new situations?

LEARNING THROUGH FEEDBACK SPIRALS

You can never step into the river of time twice.

Heroclitus

Feedback spirals are an important way organizations can achieve self-regulation. These spirals depend on a variety of information for their success. In some cases, individuals make changes after consciously observing their own feelings, attitudes, and skills. Some spirals depend on the observations of outsiders (such as "critical friends"). In other cases, those directly involved in change collect specific kinds of evidence about what is happening in the organization's environment. Once these data are analyzed, interpreted, and internalized, individuals modify their actions to more closely achieve the organization's goals. Thus, individuals—and the organization—are continually self-learning, self-renewing, and self-modifying.

Figure 3.1 (see p. 34) shows how components of a feedback spiral may be diagrammed as a recursive, cyclical pathway. Each element along the spiral is described below:

• *Clarify goals and purposes.* What is the purpose for what you are doing? What beliefs or values does it reflect? What outcomes would you expect as a result of your actions?
• *Plan.* What actions would you take to achieve the desired outcomes? How would you set up an experiment to test your ideas? What evidence would you collect to help inform you about the results of your actions? What would you look for as indicators your outcomes were or were not achieved? How will you leave the door open for other discoveries and possibilities that were not built into the original design? What process will you put in place that will help you describe what actually happened?

• *Take action/experiment.* Execute the plan.

• *Assess/gather evidence.* Implement assessment strategy.

• *Study, reflect, evaluate.* Whether this is an individual or organizational change, how are the results congruent with stated values? What meaning can be made of the data? Who might serve as a critical friend to coach, facilitate, or mediate your learning from this experience? What have individuals learned from this action?

• *Modify actions based on new knowledge.* What will be done differently in the future as a result of reflection and integration of new knowledge? Is this plan worth trying again?

• *Revisit and clarify goals and purposes.* Do the goals still make sense? Are they still of value, or do they need to be redefined, refocused, or refined? This element returns to the first step in the spiral: clarify goals and purposes.

To develop the habit of remaining open to continuous learning, the school community gathers data through conscious observation of feelings, attitudes, and skills; through observation and interviews with others; and by collecting evidence showing the effects of their efforts on the environment. These data are analyzed, interpreted, and internalized. Based on this analysis, the organization, or individuals, modify actions to more closely achieve the goals. Thus, individuals and the organization become continually self-learning, self-renewing, and self-modifying (Costa & Kallick, 1995).

MEASURING DISPOSITIONS

The habits of mind define what is meant by being "smart." Many classroom teachers have searched for ways to make those attributes visible to students and observers. For example, they invite students to describe ways to determine if they are becoming more aware of their own thinking (metacognitive). A teacher might ask, "What would it look like and sound like if you were becoming more aware of your own thinking?" Students can answer in many different ways. They can

• List the steps and tell where they are in the sequence of a problem-solving strategy.

• Trace the pathways and dead ends they took on the road to a problem solution.

• Describe the data they lack and their plans for producing them.

FIGURE 3.1
Continuous Growth Through Feedback Spirals

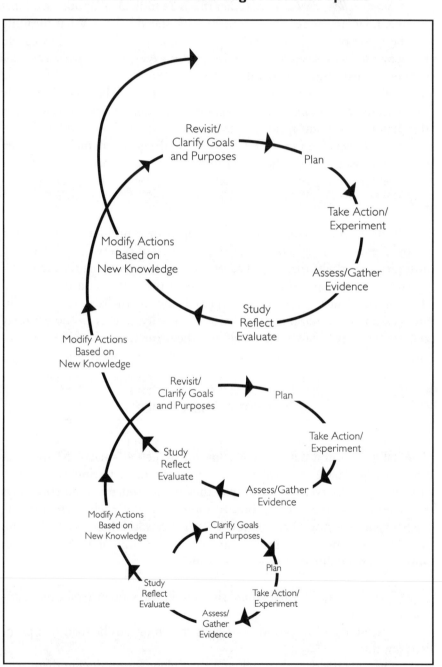

Source: Costa & Kallick, 1995, p. 27.

If students are working in the habit of persisting, you might ask, "What would we see or hear a person doing if that person is persistent?" Students might describe answers like these:

• Stick to it when the solution to a problem is not immediately apparent.
• Employ systematic methods of analyzing a problem and of determining how to begin, what steps to be performed, and when the steps are accurate or in error.
• Take pride in their efforts.
• Self-correct.
• Strive for craftsmanship and accuracy in their products and become more self-directed in problem-solving abilities.

These kinds of performance checklists are best developed through conversations in the classroom. Ask students, "What would it look like if a person were a good listener? What would it sound like if a person were a good listener?" Guide students as they generate a list of positively stated, observable behaviors. For example, in the "looks like" category, students might say, "maintains eye contact" or "nods head when agreeing." In the "sounds like" category, they might say, "builds on the other person's ideas" or "clarifies when does not understand."

Finally, the students and teacher agree to look for these behaviors. Figure 3.2 (see p. 36) shows a checklist students created for observing the habit of listening with understanding and empathy. They generated a list of what they would be observing in their own behavior as they worked with others. The checklist is used for self-evaluation to answer the question, "How am I doing?"

As students become more familiar with observing those behaviors in their own work, they often shift to a checklist for the group that they are working in. At this point, they are observing, "How are *we* doing?" The same checklist can apply for either individual or group evaluation.

This checklist is one example from a classroom. A class can prepare checklists for each of the habits as they are introduced and are pertinent to the work requirements. Students can keep a folder with the results from their checklists, each carefully dated. When reporting time comes, students can create a bar graph of each behavior and see a profile of how frequently ("often," "sometimes," "not yet") they are using the behaviors.

Once students feel comfortable assessing themselves, the teacher might ask them to rate themselves and the others in their group. Students would then compare ratings and see how accurately they perceive themselves. The teacher might also rate the students and give specific examples of how they are evidencing the positive behaviors of a particular habit.

FIGURE 3.2

Checklist for Listening with Understanding and Empathy

How Am I Doing?

Behavior	Often	Sometimes	Not Yet
Verbal			
Restates/paraphrases a person's idea before offering personal opinion.			
Clarifies a person's ideas, concepts, or terminology.			
Expresses empathy for others' feelings or emotions.			
Poses questions intended to engage thinking and reflection.			
Expresses personal regard and interest.			
Nonverbal			
Faces the person who is speaking.			
Establishes eye contact if appropriate.			
Nods head.			
Uses facial expressions congruent with speaker's emotional message.			
Mirrors gestures.			
Mirrors posture.			

As students begin to collect data about their behavior over time, they may create a graph of their progress (or lack of it!). They will find it helpful to receive feedback from their peers and their teacher in addition to their own assessment of how they are doing.

USING RUBRICS

Scoring rubrics are another way to assess the habits of mind. These rubrics also promote self-evaluation when students help develop them. Each category should be sufficiently clear so that students can learn from the feedback about their behavior and see ways to improve.

Figures 3.3–3.7 (see pp. 38–42) are examples of rubrics for several habits of mind. They were developed by educators at Tamalpais Elementary School in Mill Valley, California. After a staff meeting, teachers were to return to their classrooms and work through the rubrics, adding to and refining them so that students understood the expectations. The developmental continuum in these rubrics (from novice to expert) derives from Tech Paths for Math (Kallick & Wilson, 1997).

PORTFOLIOS

Keeping track is a matter of reflective review and summarizing in which there is both discrimination and record of the significant features of a developing experience. . . . It is the heart of intellectual organization and of the disciplined mind.

John Dewey, *Experience and Education*

Many teachers use the habits of mind as a way to organize students' portfolios. For example, the portfolio can be sectioned with folders. Label each folder with a habit of mind. Students choose work based on their best example of whatever habit they're focusing on at the time. They place the work in the portfolio in the appropriate file, and they reflect on why they chose that particular piece and what it should say to the reader of the portfolio.

Students can coach one another through peer conferences as they build these portfolios. One teacher we know asks students to read the work in a student's portfolio and help the student reflect on why that student chose a particular piece.

FIGURE 3.3
Rubric for Thinking About Thinking (Metacognition)

Level of Work	Criteria
Expert	Describes in detail the steps of thinking when solving a problem or doing other kinds of mental tasks. Explains in detail how thinking about thinking helps improve work and how it helps to develop a better learner. Describes a plan before starting to solve a problem. Monitors steps in the plan or strategy. Reflects on the efficiency of the problem-solving strategy.
Practitioner	Describes one's thinking while solving a problem or doing other kinds of mental tasks. Explains how thinking about thinking helps learning and helps to improve work.
Apprentice	Includes only sparse or incomplete information when describing how one is thinking and solving a problem or doing other kinds of mental tasks. Sees only small benefits gained from thinking about thinking and learning.
Novice	Is confused about the relationship between thinking and problem solving. Sees no relationship between thinking and learning. Is unable to describe thinking when problem solving.

Source: Tamalpais Elementary School, Mill Valley, California. Based on Marzano, Pickering, & McTighe, 1993.

When portfolios are developed around the habits of mind, the habits are transdisciplinary. This approach answers the question many teachers face about how to have one portfolio that can work across all subjects.

"This poem has no beginning" was the first line of a poem in the portfolio of Tracy from Southampton Public Schools in Southampton, New York. When asked why she wanted to enter this poem into her portfolio, she replied, "I want to be able to describe my process for developing a piece of writing." She then proceeded to describe how she often takes a walk through the woods by a stream, returns to her room, clears her desk, plays music, and starts to write. In this particular poem, she still was not feeling inspired. She sat with pen in hand and finally wrote, "This poem has no beginning," and the writing just seemed to flow from there.

Tracy was trying to describe what some might call incubation: that time when one, either consciously or preconsciously, is developing an idea. Through work with her teacher, she was brought to understand the significance of making that process of development conscious, explicit, or what

FIGURE 3.4

Rubric for Persisting

Level of Work	Criteria
Expert	Does not give up no matter how difficult it is to find the answers to solutions. Evaluates the use of a variety of strategies to stay on task.
Practitioner	Does not give up when trying to find the answers or solutions. Stays on task.
Apprentice	Tries to complete tasks when the answers or solutions are not readily available, but gives up when task is too difficult. Gets off task easily.
Novice	Gives up easily and quickly on difficult tasks.

Source: Tamalpais Elementary School, Mill Valley, California. Based on Marzano, Pickering, & McTighe, 1993.

we refer to as metacognitive. Tracy entered this piece as an example of how she had grown as a writer and how aware she was of her process for moving an idea from incubation to reality.

Amy is a 6th grade student in Mamaroneck Public Schools in Mamaroneck, New York, who was asked to choose a piece of writing for her portfolio that demonstrated her development as a problem solver. The teacher was surprised by her choice, but she better understood when she read the following reflection:

> This piece was written after my grandfather died. I was so sad that he died, and I did not know how to rid myself of the sadness. We went on a class trip, and I took photos of where we were. I placed those photos around my bed and laid on my bed for hours looking at the photos and thinking about my grandfather. Finally, I got up and wrote this piece. It shows how I was able to solve my problem of sadness through writing.

In this reflection, Amy clearly shows evidence of her disposition for problem solving and drawing from previous experiences to reflect on her learning.

When classroom communities require that students use portfolios to build narratives of their own learning, and when they focus on the opportunities for student reflection as Tracy and Amy's teachers did, the habits of

FIGURE 3.5
Rubrics for Managing Impulsivity

Level of Work	Criteria
Expert	Sets clear goals and describes each step to be taken to achieve the goals. Schedules each step and monitors progress.
Practitioner	Sets clear goals and describes some of the steps needed to achieve the goals. Also sequences some of the steps.
Apprentice	Begins to work with unclear goals. Describes only a few of the steps needed to achieve the goals. Becomes distracted from schedule.
Novice	Begins to work in random fashion. Is unclear about the goals or is unable to state the goals or outcomes or steps in achieving the goals.

Level of Work	Criteria
Expert	Evaluates a situation carefully and seeks advice from other sources to decide whether more information is needed before acting. Looks for sources of information that might help and studies them to find important information.
Practitioner	Evaluates a situation to decide if more information is needed before acting. Searches for information if needed.
Apprentice	Evaluates a situation quickly to decide if more information is needed before acting. Searches for only the most obvious information.
Novice	Acts with inadequate or incomplete information and shows little inclination to gather further data to inform decisions.

Source: Tamalpais Elementary School, Mill Valley, California. Based on Marzano, Pickering, & McTighe, 1993.

FIGURE 3.6
Rubric for Thinking Flexibly

Level of Work	CRITERIA	
	In Repertoire	**In Perspective**
Expert	Uses time and resources creatively to find as many ways as possible to look at a situation. Evaluates these many ways to see how useful they might be. Expresses appreciation for others' points of view. Changes mind and incorporates others' points of view in own thinking.	Consistently explores as many alternatives as time and resources will allow and analyzes how the identified alternatives will affect outcomes. The alternatives illustrate extremely diverse but highly useful ways of looking at situations.
Practitioner	Finds a variety of ways to look at a situation and evaluates how useful they are. Describes some ways others' points of view are found to be new and different from own perspective.	Consistently generates alternative ways of approaching tasks and analyzes how the alternatives will affect those tasks. Some alternatives show originality in the approach to the tasks.
Apprentice	Describes different ways of looking at a situation from own perspective.	Sporadically generates alternative ways of approaching tasks and analyzes how the alternatives will affect those tasks. Some alternatives show originality in the approach to the tasks.
Novice	Looks at a situation in only one way, and that way often is one's own. Looks no further even when it is clear that doing so would be helpful.	Rarely generates alternative ways of approaching tasks. The few alternatives lack originality.

Source: Tamalpais Elementary School, Mill Valley, California. Based on Marzano, Pickering, & McTighe, 1993.

FIGURE 3.7
Rubric for Group Cooperation

Level of Work	Group Criteria
4	Demonstrates interdependence. Shows contributions from all members. Shows indicators of cooperation and working together, compromising, and staying on task. Welcomes disagreements as learning opportunities. Completes task with accuracy and within time limits. Listens to others' points of view. Shows evidence of paraphrasing, clarifying, and empathizing.
3	Reaches agreements through arguing and debate. Shows evidence of some paraphrasing and clarifying. Sometimes strays from task. Shows evidence of some members remaining silent or refraining from participating.
2	Demonstrates some off-task behavior. Rushes to complete task in the most expedient way because of time limits. Argues or encourages members to get task over with.
I	Demonstrates little on-task behavior. Argues and shows disinterest.
0	Shows chaos. Does not complete task. Engages in put-downs. Reduces group size because of members leaving. Complains about having to participate in task.

Source: Tamalpais Elementary School, Mill Valley, California. Based on Marzano, Pickering, & McTighe, 1993.

mind are a powerful frame to guide them through their work. Teachers and students often ask, "What goes into a portfolio?" A better question is, "What will be the frame or structure of the portfolio?"

In Kathleen Reilly's 10th and 12th grade English classes at Edgemont High School in Edgemont, New York, the students' portfolios are framed with the habits of mind. Each student has a list of the habits permanently fixed to the inside of the portfolio cover. Students also work with checklists that help them look at the habits of mind in their work.

Their work with the habits begins with the teacher's response to individual essays on the specific terms of persistence, precision, and accuracy. In the space at the bottom of a checklist, students are asked to choose which of those habits of mind they think will help them write better essays.

Later in the school year, students are pushed further in their reflections about essays. They must ask peers to assume the role of coach. For example, 10th grader Sam tells Michael that Michael's essay illustrates his flexibility in thinking when he "uses many metaphors for the journey: development, emotional progression, humility." Sam also notes how Michael's precision of language shows in his "good use of synonyms." After he reads Sam's reflection, Michael notes that he can improve his essay "by listening to others—taking fellow students' advice to heart." He adds that he will get better at this writing stuff when he "applies metacognition, . . . trying to understand how I came to my thesis and prove it."

In Reilly's class, stretching the habits of mind to serve as a structural frame for character analysis was a natural outgrowth of earlier work. Students could not resist writing about character strengths and weaknesses. Working with 10th graders on *Huckleberry Finn*, Reilly created portfolio assignments that asked direct questions about the students' thinking patterns, the intellectual and emotional choices of the literary characters, and the way the students thought about their essays. Overall, the habits of mind provided a sensitive structure to the portfolio. Students easily adapted to the list, and they made connections to specific instances in the novel as well as to their own lives. Here are some questions Reilly asked about the novel:

• What specific habits of mind are apparent in this character? Cite scenes where you recognize the habits of mind.
• How could this character have behaved more intelligently?
• What possible alternative strategies could this character have used to solve problems?

Reilly uses a reflection/response form to give students the choice of character to think about. Although many chose to analyze Huck, Tom, or Jim, others were drawn to negative characters: Pap, the King, and the Duke. Just the task of "thinking about thinking" initiated conversations about Twain's intention in creating characters to educate and challenge Huck.

Specifically, although Huck was unanimously credited with possessing persistence and creativity, students sharply criticized him for his lack of flexibility in thinking about Jim, for not listening to others, and for not reflecting. As John put it, "One of Huck's major problems is his . . . trouble seeing Jim and all blacks outside of the prejudices existing in society. Huck needs to think outside this mind-set."

Centering on an analysis of the King, Tina found his major faults were in "being overly impulsive. . . . He started schemes without thinking."

Another question pushed students to think about their own process of arriving at conclusions about characters. Beverly wrote, "I tried to put myself in his shoes, to think about how I would react." Tina wrote, "I thought about each habit and tried to apply it to the King. . . . [If] I wasn't sure, I tried to apply each trait to a real-life example to see how the King would react." By the end of the year, students went back through their portfolio and saw how easily they talked about literature in terms of the habits of mind.

Although Reilly teaches English, she asked students to include in their portfolios writing examples from other classes. What followed were discussions of audiences, the styles and expectations of other disciplines, and the ways that a powerful voice can be heard in every piece of writing. The examples gave insight into the possibilities of using the habits of mind as a transdisciplinary frame with students completing a portfolio representing their work in several subjects.

*   *   *

Portfolios can help us continuously recreate the narrative of our own learning. All the failures and misfires are in a portfolio, sitting right next to the triumphs and breakthroughs! Peers cheer the growth they see, the power of words selected, and the essays they wish they had written. Students delight in their changes, cherish the praise, and work even harder to produce an admirable product. Beyond the chronological history of work produced, the portfolio reveals a deeper layer where the patterns of work tell a personal story of a student's learning. The habits of mind serve as a powerful framework for this work.

PERFORMANCES

Teachers become increasingly aware of the significance of habits of mind when students prepare presentations of their work. These performances require orchestration and a great deal of social thinking. Students can receive feedback about the habits of mind during three parts of the performance:

- When they are planning for a performance.
- When they are in the process of working on the performance.
- When they are presenting their work to an audience.

DURING PLANNING

A science teacher sets a challenge to his students. They must work together to create a persuasive presentation to the class about a solution to a particular ecological problem. He asks the students to choose one habit they feel especially strong in and one that they need to work on. They then plan how they will work to develop the habits through the actions they take. Next they develop a list of indicators as a group: What will a habit look like when we see it happening? They agree to keep records of when they observe the use of a habit. What is important about this process is that they plan to pay attention to the habits of mind *before* they begin their work.

DURING THE PROCESS

Record-keeping forms are useful for students to document their observations about the habits of mind. In one high school class, students keep a log of their process during project development. Group members rotate responsibility for log entries for each day that they are working together. They reflect on

1. What did we learn today?
2. What did we notice about the way the group is working?
3. What did the group and group member do to contribute to the group's success?
4. What might we do to be more effective as a group?
5. Which habits of mind would help us to be more productive?

DURING THE PRESENTATION

During a presentation, students are required to focus on striving for accuracy; thinking and communicating with clarity and precision; creating, imagining, innovating; questioning and posing problems; and thinking about thinking (metacognition). The audience is asked to pay attention to the accuracy of the information. They also take note of the use of proper terminology. Figure 3.8 (see p. 46) shows an example of a rubric developed by educators in the Mamaroneck Public Schools for judging the quality of a 6th grade exhibition.

In a book by Wasley and her colleagues, Wasley discusses the gains that students have made as a result of developing exhibitions. She states,

> We saw young people like Tommy, Sean, and Hakim discover topics of interest and develop them over time so that they build legitimate skills, recognized by adults and other students—recognition they would not have easily obtained had the school not changed its requirements. We saw evidence that students understood important concepts thoroughly and could apply them in new circumstances: math in building boats,

FIGURE 3.8
Rubric for Personal Exhibit Assessment

6th Grade Exhibition

Presenter's Name: _____

Scorer's Name: _____

Date of Presentation: _____

Scoring Criteria	Clear 3	Moderate 2	Not Quite 1
Through this exhibit, the creator demonstrates the following: That she/he is a successful PROBLEM SOLVER 1. Defines the problem.			
2. Brainstorms/thinks of possible solutions.			
3. Persists to find a solution.			
4. Takes action.			
That she/he is a thorough RESEARCHER 5. Raises questions/chooses topics to research.			
6. Knows where to look for information.			
7. Uses a variety of sources.			
8. Takes time to be thoughtful.			
9. Organizes the data.			
10. Checks for accuracy of information.			
That she/he is an effective COMMUNICATOR 11. Uses his/her own voice (words) to express ideas.			
12. Uses feedback to strengthen his/her work.			
13. Final product communicates in an organized and meaningful way to the audience—ideas are clear and easily understood.			
Her/His PLAQUES: 14. Reflect on strategies and process.			
15. SHOW GROWTH in all areas.			
Please write further comments below. Your words are very important!			

Source: Central Elementary School, Mamaroneck, New York.

data gathering and analysis in forecasting weather, electronics in wiring car radios. We noted gains that were embedded in students' abilities to work on a particular topic over time. They demonstrated persistence— an important ability in nearly all walks of life. Tanya, whose parents were recovering addicts, ran the data over and over again in order to make sure her findings were correct, and then she ran them again with a new set of variables. We saw papers, videos, speeches that were rehearsed and nearly errorless, because students had developed a consciousness of audience and correctness (Wasley, Hempel, & Clark, 1997, p. 201).

ANECDOTAL RECORDS

As teachers strive to be constantly alert to students' demonstration of the habits of mind, they document student work. The most significant part of this strategy is to be systematic about record keeping. One teacher found that she was able to observe all the children in her class when she designed a special notebook. She tabbed each section with a student's name and used sticky notes to jot down information when students demonstrated various habits of mind. When she wanted to write narrative comments about students at the end of the first marking period, she had a good pool of data from which to draw.

Parents and caregivers can also be asked to record students' growth. Many teachers send a copy of the habits of mind home and ask parents to notice when the child is using the behaviors in the home environment. When conference time comes, the parents share their observations with the teacher. Figure 3.9 (see p. 48) shows a tool that educators in Maple Valley, Washington, use to encourage parents to track how students demonstrate thinking behaviors. Parents also receive a two-page guide explaining how they can strengthen students' thinking behaviors.

Besides documenting performances, teachers are also alert to students' comments before, during, and after learning activities, projects, and assignments. Students often reveal their awareness, understanding, and application of the habits of mind as they plan for and reflect on their work. Here are student comments about the habits of mind collected by Michele Swanson at Sir Francis Drake High School in San Anselmo, California:

Persisting. "In the last project when I couldn't have been more stressed, I wanted to quit and walk away, but no matter how much I wanted to give up because I had no idea what I was doing or how it was going to be done, no matter how much I wanted to throw the Makita because it wasn't work-

FIGURE 3.9
12 Ways Your Child or Student Shows Growth in Thinking Skills

This is a parent/teacher tool for rating a student's home/school thinking behaviors at the beginning and end of a school year. It should identify student strengths and weaknesses and promote some parent/teacher "team" goal setting to help the student develop more successful thinking strategies.

Mark each behavior using N = Not Yet; S = Sometimes; F = Frequently

During the _____ school year, I notice that

Name: _____ Age: _____ does the following:

	PARENT		TEACHER		Behavior
	Fall	Spring	Fall	Spring	
1.					Keeps trying; does not give up easily.
2.					Shows less impulsivity; thinks more before answering a question.
3.					Listens to others with understanding and empathy.
4.					States several ways to solve a problem (shows flexibility in thinking).
5.					Puts into words how he/she solved a problem; is aware of his/her own thinking.
6.					Checks for accuracy and precision; checks completed work without being asked.
7.					Asks questions; wants to find out new information.
8.					Uses knowledge already learned in new situations; can solve problems in everyday living like using allowance, taking messages, going to the store, and practicing safety.
9.					Uses words more carefully to describe feelings, wants, and other things.
10.					Uses touch, taste, smell, sound, and sight to learn. Enjoys music, art, experimenting, and active play.
11.					Enjoys making and doing original things; likes to show individuality in thought and dress.
12.					Enjoys problem solving, curiosity, wonderment, and inquisitiveness.

Source: Tahoma School District, Maple Valley, Washington.

ing, no matter how much responsibility I was forced to take on, I stuck with it until the end, always knowing (hoping) it would turn out great."

Listening with understanding and empathy. "Listening before prejudging someone's contribution makes sense. Being patient helps. I was surprised at the great ideas and how much everyone added."

Finding humor. "Getting to know these people can really impact your life and your work very positively, so you always have to keep a light and open heart, and humor can aid in this." Also, "Humor keeps people relaxed and much more comfortable even while working on serious subject matter."

Thinking about thinking (metacognition). "I sometimes have to talk to myself and tell myself to work harder, or to stop slacking." Also, "They give us time to think about everything—all of our actions and work and that is something that really helps. Not many kids get that; it's so neat."

Thinking interdependently. "It's not about what you want or somebody else does. It's about working as a team to get the job done." Also, "At first, I was not a good group worker because I felt controlling and perfectionist. I had to step back and examine my thinking and adjust to be cooperative and open. I changed the way I thought about my role in the group process."

Questioning and posing problems. "Asking the right questions is very helpful in order to learn how to use the equipment effectively."

Applying past knowledge to new situations. "Every time I finished a project, I was able to enter the next one with more knowledge of the group process. Also, with each project I became more technologically advanced, which helped me add value to the group."

Striving for accuracy. "Our venue was four minutes long. After every four minutes, I had to move everything back to the original spot in one minute. Every single little thing had to be perfect."

INTERVIEWS

Oprah Winfrey, Larry King, and Barbara Walters are all master interviewers. They have the capacity to place the most timid person at ease by creating trust and rapport, and they have developed the skills to lead the most reticent guest to reveal that person's deepest emotions and secrets. Teachers, too, can use interviews to lead students to share their reflections about the habits of mind. For example, you might consider posing such questions as these:

• As you reflect on this semester's work, which of the habits of mind were you most aware of in your own learnings?

• Which habit of mind will you focus your energies on as you begin our next project?

• What insights have you gained as a result of employing these habits of mind?

• As you think about your future, how might these habits of mind be used as a guide in your life?

Interviews provide teachers with opportunities to model the habits of listening with understanding and empathy, thinking and communicating with clarity and precision, and questioning and posing problems. Teaching students to conduct interviews provides situations in which they must also practice these habits of mind. The ultimate purpose of interviewing, though, is to lead students to another powerful strategy: the self-interview.

JOURNALS AND LOGS

Consciousness about the habits of mind often begins with journal entries designed to help students focus on how they are developing. Learning logs and journals are a way to integrate content, process, personal feelings, and the habits of mind. They are especially powerful in engaging metacognition and helping students to draw forth previous knowledge.

Before, or directly following, a unit, project, or area of study, invite students to make entries in their logs or journals. Short, frequent bursts of writing are sometimes more productive than infrequent, longer assignments. Teachers, too, can join in the writing process by reflecting on their teaching, analyzing learners' learning, preserving anecdotes about the class interactions, and projecting ideas for how they might approach a unit of study differently in the future.

Sometimes you'll hear students complain, "I don't know what to write." To stimulate thinking, post questioning stems on a chart or in the front of the log or journals. Consider these sentence starters to help students use the habits of mind as a way of documenting their learning:

• One thing that surprised me today was . . .
• I felt particularly flexible when I . . .
• I used my senses to . . .
• As I think about how I went about solving the problem, I . . .
• A question I want to pursue is . . .

• When I checked my work I found . . .
• Because I listened carefully I learned . . .

You can collect specific log entries from time to time, read through them, and share written comments with students. This practice helps build stronger relationships with the learners and provides a useful way to informally assess how well they are doing and how their conscious use of the habits of mind is developing.

Add annotated journal or log entries to portfolios. Invite students to choose an entry from the beginning, middle, and end of the learning period. These entries can be included in a final portfolio along with the student's reflections and synthesis connecting the entries or general comments about learning over time (Lipton, 1997).

Not all habits of mind are assessed using the same techniques. Figure 3.10 (see pp. 52–53) might serve as a form for you to use in developing assessment strategies for your school and classroom. We designed the matrix in the figure to help you plan a balance of assessment strategies across several habits of mind.

REFERENCES

Costa, A., & Kallick, B. (1995). *Assessment in the learning organization: Shifting the paradigm.* Alexandria, VA: Association for Supervision and Curriculum Development.

Kallick, B., & Wilson, J. (1997). *Tech paths for math: An assessment management system for your classroom.* Amherst, MA: Technology Pathways Corp.

Lipton, L. (1997). *50 ways to literacy.* Arlington Heights, IL: Skylight Publishers.

Marzano, R., Pickering, D., & McTighe, J. (1993). *Assessing student outcomes: Performance assessment using the Dimensions of Learning model.* Alexandria, VA: Association for Supervision and Curriculum Development.

Wasley, P., Hempel, R. & Clark, R. (1997). *Kids and school reform.* San Francisco: Jossey-Bass.

FIGURE 3.10

Planning Matrix for Collecting Evidence

Habit of Mind	Checklist	Portfolio	Rubric	Interview	Anecdotal	Performance	Exhibition	Journal
1. Persisting								
2. Managing impulsivity								
3. Listening with understanding and empathy								
4. Thinking flexibly								
5. Thinking about thinking (metacognition)								
6. Striving for accuracy								
7. Questioning and posing problems								
8. Applying past knowledge to new situations								

TYPE OF ASSESSMENT

FIGURE 3.10—continued
Planning Matrix for Collecting Evidence

TYPE OF ASSESSMENT

Habit of Mind	Checklist	Portfolio	Rubric	Interview	Anecdotal	Performance	Exhibition	Journal
9. Thinking and communicating with clarity and precision								
10. Gathering data through all senses								
11. Creating, imagining, innovating								
12. Responding with wonderment and awe								
13. Taking responsible risks								
14. Finding humor								
15. Thinking interdependently								
16. Remaining open to continuous learning								

In this chapter, Steve Seidel presents a powerful integration of the use of the habits of mind as teachers study student work. In addition to using a specific protocol to facilitate the careful study of student work, he guides the conversation with such habits as questioning and posing problems and responding with wonderment and awe. He describes a carefully facilitated environment where teachers learn to trust one another and, especially, to trust their "wondering."

—Arthur L. Costa and Bena Kallick

WONDERING TO BE DONE

STEVE SEIDEL

I remember meditating on these attached objects. . . . (feet and hands, especially, but also chest, knees, stomach) . . . looking at them, touching them, feeling them from the outside and from the inside, wondering about them because there was wondering to be done, not because there were answers to be found.

Jane Smiley, *A Thousand Acres*

Several years ago, I spent three months conducting a series of workshops with 10 teachers from Fuller Elementary School in Gloucester, Massachusetts. When the final session was over, I began a long period of wondering about the value of the work we'd just completed.[1] Our work

Adapted by permission of the publisher from Allen, D. (Ed.), *Assessing student learning: From grading to understanding* (New York: Teachers College Press, © 1998 by Teachers College, Columbia University. All rights reserved), pp. 21–39.

[1]Thanks to the Lilly Endowment, The Pew Charitable Trusts, and the Rockefeller Foundation for support of this research. I also offer thanks to the educators at Fuller Elementary who supported this work: Bill Bruns, Julie Carter, Pamela Card, Ellen Sibley, Margaret Wilmot, Alyce McMenimen, Elizabeth Parillo, Nancy Rhodes, Cherylann Parker, Ron Eckel, Sheila Callahan-Young, and Annette Boothroyd. Also, thanks to Jessica Brennan and her family for permission to use her poem and illustration.

had gone well in so many ways. We enjoyed ourselves and remained engaged with our task. Final evaluations were strongly positive, pointing to many lessons and benefits for the participating teachers.

So why did I doubt?

Our workshops were conducted in five sessions. Four lasted four hours; the final session was a two-hour reflection. The task was to explore the benefits and difficulties of working with a protocol for examining children's work, called collaborative assessment conferences. This protocol had been designed by my colleagues at Harvard Project Zero and myself during our work in the Pittsburgh Public Schools on Arts Propel (Seidel, 1998). Each participating teacher shared a piece of writing from a K–5 student, and we followed the conference structure to consider the student's work.

The conference protocol called for extensive examination and description of each work. Over the three months, we read and talked about 10 pieces of student writing. What a luxurious experience! Four hours at a time just to look at and talk about student work! There were no placement decisions to make, no scores to decide on, no remedial plans to hammer out. It was a situation so out of character from the way professional time is usually spent in most schools that virtually everyone participating was, at times, ill at ease.

Still, our work progressed, and in time, some interesting things began to happen. Reflecting on the first conference, Julie noted the effect of considering student work collaboratively: "It made me see a lot more than I would just sitting alone. And the more you looked, the more you saw." These comments seemed true to me; I had noticed that the teachers' first hesitant observations led slowly but surely into a sequence of more and more specific descriptions. It wasn't until the sessions were completed that the consequences of this phenomenon became clearer to me.

As I reviewed the workshops, I noticed certain patterns in our conversations. The more the teachers looked at a piece of student writing, the more they recognized the complexity of the child's effort and accomplishments. As they grappled with the complexity of the work, they became even more interested in the child who created it. The more interested they became in the child, the more they wanted to meet and talk with the child. They generated questions that only the young author could answer. The teachers deeply wanted those answers, and they wanted to get to know the child, too.

With all these positive outcomes, why did I still wonder about the value of our experiences? Perhaps it was because I kept hearing one of the workshop teachers, Elizabeth, asking how our work would translate into something positive for her students. Liz raised this question several times in the course of the meetings, both orally and in her written reflections, and

I always felt inadequate trying to answer her. I didn't know if sitting together for so many hours talking about specific pieces of writing would translate into something positive for her students. What meaning would these teachers make of the workshops, and what would they take back to their classrooms?

I did notice that as the sessions progressed, Liz became very involved with our discussions. At one point, she wrote about one effect these sessions were having on her:

> [It may be] off the subject, but I'm aware of how alive I feel when I am part of a conversation [or] discussion about *language*—I like to be reminded about possibilities and options—offering the child options—seeing possibilities in writing. There doesn't have to be a definitive answer—*so* different from when I *was* a student [emphasis in original].

Liz seemed torn between her sense of responsibility to her students and her enjoyment of our work. She deeply believed that if she was not in class with students, she should be doing something that clearly would benefit them. In retrospect, I suspect that in the high-stakes, outcome-based world of education and professional development, I heard Liz's very real and very serious question—"How will my students benefit from this?"—and felt insecure about what I really believed. Though I shared my thoughts with that group, I was not confident.

I've spent the last several years engaging many more teachers in regular sessions devoted to collaboratively looking at pieces of student work. I better understand the value of that activity and the protocol we use. In short, I've come to believe that the protocol encourages a sense of wonder: about children, writing, teaching, curriculum, assessment, and more. And, like Jane Smiley's narrator in *A Thousand Acres*, I've found value in wondering because "there was wondering to be done, not because there were answers to be found."

THE PROTOCOL STEPS

The collaborative assessment conference protocol has a series of distinct sections and basic guidelines. Briefly, the protocol follows this structure:

1. *Read the text.* In silence, everyone reads a student text that has been brought to the session by a participant who has agreed to be the "presenting" teacher for the conference.

2. *Observe and describe.* The presenting teacher remains silent. All other participants discuss the work, and they focus first, as strictly as possible, on a description of the piece.

3. *Raise questions.* Description is followed by articulation of questions about the text, the author, or the context of the writing.

4. *What is the child working on?* The readers speculate on what they think the child was working on as the child created the text.

5. *The presenting teacher responds.* Throughout the discussion so far, the presenting teacher has been silent. At this point, the presenting teacher adds personal observations about the text, answering as many questions as possible.

6. *Teaching moves and pedagogical responses.* Together, the readers and presenting teacher consider possible teaching moves to encourage and challenge the writer.

7. *Reflection.* When all this conversation is complete, the entire group, including the facilitator, reflects on the conference. They consider its satisfactions, frustrations, and confusions as well as ways to improve the next conference.

In addition to prescribing when the presenting teacher should listen and speak, the protocol has two major guidelines or rules. First, participants are asked to withhold their judgments of the work under consideration. This restraint includes expressions of taste ("I like [or don't like] ____ about the work") or of quality ("This is [or isn't] good"). Second, in the initial phases of the conference, as little information as possible is revealed about the writer and the context of the writing (such as assignment, grade, gender, or materials provided). These guidelines make collaborative assessment conferences quite different from most forms of assessment regularly practiced by teachers.

Furthermore, most teachers rarely experience any form of structured and regular professional conversations about specific pieces of children's work. It is hardly ever part of regular staff discussion, inservice programs, or most teacher training courses. In this light, the Gloucester workshops, focused and structured as they were, were an extraordinary professional experience for these teachers. Without making specific claims for their value, it is reasonable to suggest that the focus and structure of these workshops were a radical departure from the ordinary.

A Conference in Action

Following is an account of one piece of student work we considered during the Gloucester workshops and the first from a 1st grade classroom. This was the eighth piece of student work we had discussed together. The text is briefer than a full transcript, but it does represent the flow and focus of the session.

After we settled in, Julie and Pam handed out copies of "May Is" for everyone to read. Before continuing with this chapter, stop and read "May Is" in Figure 4.1. Reading this work carefully before going any further will help you understand the discussion that follows. (You might even want to read the work aloud.)

Figure 4.1

May Is

Julie had agreed to take the role of the facilitator for this conference, and Pam was the presenting teacher. Julie gave people several minutes to read and reread the text and to consider the picture. After Julie called for observations and descriptions, it didn't take long for the teachers to raise the issue of punctuation in the piece or, more correctly, the lack of punctuation.

The teachers noted the ambiguity of the author's meaning. Ellen said, "To me, it [the text] is a child brainstorming the world going on around them or feelings about the month of May, which is 'bees in flowers' and 'birds in the sky.'"

Alyce jumped in, "Or 'sky dogs walking flowers'! That's what I see."

Cherylann was first to point to the lack of punctuation: "I don't see any punctuation, and I see an interesting choice of word placement that sometimes doesn't reflect whether the child has sentence structure, such as the whole idea of 'butterflies dancing in the sky dogs walking flowers. . . .' or is it 'dogs walking. flowers that are blue and red.' There isn't a real finite way of knowing where things stop and start."

Throughout this conference, the issue of no punctuation, and the subsequent ambiguity of the phrasing in the piece, came up time and again, through and around observations, as part of questions and speculations. We talked about the relationship of the text to the picture and the process through which this work came to be. We commented on the child's spelling and questions about the ending. (The child appears to have written and erased "thats the end" after "two lips" in Line 4. This erasure cannot be seen in this book, but it's evident on the original work.) There was extensive discussion about whether or not this was a poem. But the dominant concern was over how to read the meaning of these words and phrases without any punctuation to guide the way. Here is the discussion:

Annette: I want to know why the writer stopped at "two lips." It seems like there should be more to this. Unless . . .

Cherylann: Maybe the dogs are blue and red.

Annette: The dogs are walking flowers that are blue and red tulips.

A short time later, Margaret came back to the final phrases of the piece.

Margaret: I have a meaning question. Is it "flowers that are blue and red, tulips" or "flowers that are blue and red tulips"? And if you put an exclamation point on it, it would make a meaning to the whole poem.

Annette: If you are interpreting it by the picture, it looks like she is saying "flowers that are red and blue" and "tulips" is another thought.

Liz: Is the tulip made of red and blue?

Annette: No, it's purple.

Later, someone questioned how the child could mean "in the sky dogs walking flowers," and Cherylann offered that it made sense to her. Upon reading those lines, she had imagined looking up at a sky full of clouds and seeing "dogs walking flowers" in the ever-changing cloud formations. Alyce wanted to see "all of us put in the punctuation we think should go in here. We'd come up with seven or nine different pieces."

Because Julie seemed to be handling the role of the facilitator quite comfortably, I decided I could participate in this conference as a reader. I had been quiet for some time, but in examining the poem, I made a discovery that startled me. I had noted earlier that the child had written "thats the end" in Line 4 after "two lips" and then erased it. Somehow, this observation, and my own confusion over why this child had broken the lines where she did, led me to count the syllables in each line.

"I noticed [something]. . . ," I said. "I did this quickly counting on my fingers. There are four lines. I didn't have to use my fingers for that, but there are 10 syllables in Lines 1, 3, and 4, if you count 'thats the end', which the writer has taken out, and 11 [syllables] in Line 2."

This observation was striking to others as well, and it immediately raised questions about whether the number of syllables was an accident or intentional. What implications did the syllables have for whether or not this was a poem? Could this young child have actually counted the syllables? Could she have known that syllabification is an established way many poets determine where to break the lines of their poems? Could she have "invented" this poetic form? Or was this syllabification simply an accident? As usual, we reached no clear conclusions. The discussion proceeded and explored questions about the nature of the assignment. (Could the child have been told to go outside and observe nature on a recent May day?) The group jumped back and forth between observations and thoughts about the feeling of the piece and its structural components (e.g., punctuation, line breaks, and use of conjunctions).

Finally, it was Pam's turn to speak, and she was quick to note that in September this child was writing complete sentences with punctuation. "As a matter of fact, the poetry piece I had her do before last time was much more sentence oriented. Less free flowing. It was interesting to me that she broke out of that mold." Julie asked Pam to say more about this. "She was very much into a prose mold. Here's my complete thought, and this is the ending. This strikes me as atypical of her work."

Pam added that "two lips" was, indeed, meant to be tulips, and that the last line should be read as "flowers that are red and blue [pause] tulips." Pam reported that she had heard the writer read this poem aloud, and her reading of the final line made clear where the pause should be.

TEACHING MOVES AND RESPONSES

After considerable conversation about the child and her relationship to this piece of work, to writing in general, and to Pam, Julie decided it was time to move on to a discussion of teaching moves and responses. I include here a significant portion of the transcript of that part of the conference because it touches on so many issues that seem central to where the group had come by this point, our next-to-last session:

Julie: Pam, what did you do or might you do in relation to this?

Pam: With this particular piece of work, I'm not sure because where it wasn't an assignment [it was done during free-choice time], I don't know that she should touch it. Perhaps I'd have her work on commas.

Steve: To me the question is to think back to, What did I say? What was my response?

Pam: Thinking back, I wonder if she wanted to share it with the class. I could go back and offer her a chance to do that.

Nancy: I would think the very last thing you would want to do is punctuate [this piece].

Pam: No. I don't want to touch this. But I do want to talk about the use of commas in future work. No, I wouldn't touch this.

Liz: You might show her some poetry and how it is put in lines. She might want to put this in more standard form of poetic lines.

Steve: Except I think . . .

Liz: It might help with the meaning. There is still some confusion for me.

Cherylann: But the various meanings were really interesting.

Liz: Well, what is the problem then? The value is in the meaning for us, or is the value in the meaning they want to have?

Steve: Well, would that be a response? To say, hey, I can read this in two different ways. I can read this and it means "dogs walking flowers" and that makes me laugh or as "dogs walking [pause] flowers that are blue." Just to let her know that when you write poetry this way it has an ambiguity that is playful.

Liz: I like that approach better than the way . . . my approach was more clinical.

In the midst of this interchange, Liz posed a question that I take as central to this whole enterprise. In essence, she asked, "Whose meaning matters? The writer's or the reader's?" During discussion of a piece called "Beautiful Butterfly" in our third session, Cherylann had talked about the writer's voice and the reader's voice. She named the issue but didn't really push the question. The problem was complicated for these teachers. If the job of a writing teacher is to help children communicate clearly and effectively what they mean to say, how might the teacher attend to both the child's intent and the meaning the teacher makes from the text? This question is further complicated by recognizing the remarkable variety of meanings that could be drawn from a single text.

In retrospect, it is no surprise that Liz raised this question when we were talking about teaching moves. Just a bit later, Margaret picked up on this issue of multiple meanings: "If you are to read it aloud and say there are lots of ways of looking at this, it opens up for a writer a different way of looking at their work. It would be interesting to see if the child saw other ways."

TALKING ABOUT THE CONVERSATION

The last step in the protocol is to conclude the discussion of teaching moves, thank the presenting teacher for sharing the work with the group, and make sure everyone is prepared to move from talking about the work in question to talking about the conversation about the work. Julie felt it was time to move on. She checked with the group, and getting consent, she moved into the reflection on the conference.

"All I can say is whatever you are doing, you are doing a great job because when she [Pam's student, Jessica] left me at the end of last year, she couldn't do this. Bits of it, maybe, but not all of this. So I applaud you," said Alyce, starting off the reflection.

Pam took a turn to talk about her experience of the discussion. Frustration was the first thing she expressed: "That was really hard not to talk, and I felt a lot of time was wasted on 'tulips.' If I could have just said, 'this is how she meant it!' The tulip conversation was okay that it went that way, but at the time it seemed like wasted time. And I just wanted to say, 'flowers that are red and blue [pause] tulips!' And get on to the next thing!"

Pam's comments were followed by some silence, so Julie asked if there were any other thoughts about the process. I felt obliged to defend, or at least explain, why I tolerate and even encourage the kind of wasted time Pam described. I had talked before about this kind of conference as a practice, something that might be done regularly as a part of keeping one's clinical eye focused and keen.

"You are practicing your ability to wonder about children's work," I said. "It is an exercise in living with the idea that there isn't one right answer and [in] entertaining the [multiple] possibilities. I think there is some value in that even if, in the end, you tell us what the child meant and we accept that."

Annette responded by commenting on how the child's reason for writing might affect the way the teacher chooses to respond to the ambiguity or lack of clarity in the writing. The rest of the conversation picked up and pursued these themes:

Cherylann: But in terms of the process, if Pam had clarified the question and we'd never had the conversation about what to say to that child about the ambiguity . . . And what I take away from this conversation is that the next time a child comes to me with a poem, I may say, "Hey, this is really ambiguous. Did you mean that? Do you mean it to be this way?" Talking about the process, if you had clarified it beforehand, we never would have discussed the issue of ambiguity.

Margaret: I agree. And I think one of the most wonderful things you can say to a child about their work is, "I thought about this. And in my thinking I can see all different kinds of meanings." And that ambiguity is part of the richness. That it can mean one thing to the person who wrote it and something equally rich and equally meaningful to someone else. Isn't that wonderful? That kind of richness of experience.

Steve: Why do you think that's wonderful?

Margaret: I think that's wonderful because it is telling the person that wrote it that there are more things in heaven and earth than they can see. Something that they have written has more meanings than they meant. It also has meanings for others that might be different. Their experience has made it one meaning, and my experience has made it another meaning. And that's not to say that my meaning is right. A piece is very rich when there are lots of meanings. Language is very flexible.

Cherylann: But it also carries into other forms. Right now I'm concentrating on the science fair. If a child came up with ambiguous language in that, there would be a problem. Sometimes ambiguity is appropriate and fine, but not in science writing. Sometimes you need concise, precise language.

Julie: What I think is important about going back to the child and saying that "I've been thinking about your work" is the message that "You matter to me. And your work matters, and you are on my mind and you exist in my mind when you are not with me."

Liz: "And I respect you. . . ."

Julie: "And I respect you enough to think about you or your problem or your work. . . ."

Margaret: That's why I think your immediate reaction may just be, "Oh, that's very interesting." But if you come back with, "There are a lot of meanings here, and I wonder what you meant. . . ."

Liz: It shows you are really interested in their learning.

I have included this rather lengthy account of a collaborative assessment conference to provide an example of how questions emerge in the course of these conversations and the way in which a genuine interest in the child writer can grow from examining the meaning of the text. Questions, in this case, are both an expression of interest and a means by which to explore one's curiosity.

Where Do Questions Come From?

Questions come from becoming curious about something that has engaged our attention. It is a curious phenomenon that we often have difficulty staying interested in things about which we believe we know everything— or nothing at all. To become engaged with something, it helps to have some, but not too much, familiarity with the subject. Like works of art, the things children make can be highly engaging. They can captivate, confuse, charm, and alarm us. But if we think we know everything about children, their work, or a particular child, we won't watch with such care. The protocol is a trick, then, to focus attention and encourage engagement.

Questions come from engagement and from having our perceptions challenged. I believe three elements of the collaborative assessment conference protocol combine to encourage engagement:

- Withholding context.
- Withholding judgments.
- Hearing your colleagues describe what they see on the page (and in turn saying what you see).

WITHHOLDING CONTEXT

Perhaps the most fundamental beliefs underlying collaborative assessment conferences are (1) that the work children produce is worthy of serious consideration and analysis and (2) that in that work we can see much about children and their interactions with the environments in which they produced the work (the classroom, school, family, and community). Most readers, given information about a child and her context for producing a piece of writing, will view that child's work through the lens of that information; they won't let a picture of the child emerge from the work itself. Teachers often adjust their expectations of work based on their associations to the bits of information they have about a child (usually things like age, gender, grouping in school, neighborhood, native language, and socioeconomic background).

Nothing is surprising about such interpretation. Taking small clues about people and making assumptions about who they are is one way in which we all negotiate our way through a complex world. The problem for teachers is that our associations often mislead us, and they might actually blind us to important aspects of a child's character and learning.

In describing group examinations of children's writing at the Bread Loaf School of English, Armstrong addressed the effect of knowing the context of the writing on a reader's investigation of the text:

> So we begin by immersing ourselves in the text. It doesn't always pay at first to know too much about the child who wrote it or the circumstances of its composition. As Geoff Keith said in our class the other day, the trouble with concentrating on the child rather than the story is that "it allows you to marginalize the text." . . . All the time we're trying to

concentrate our whole attention on the significance of the words on the page (Armstrong, 1992, p. 3).

One of the central goals of this protocol is to encourage direct engagement between teachers and student texts with little context about the child or the assignment. As one of the Gloucester teachers said, we were focusing on "the actual writing itself." Of course, much of this contextual information is revealed in the course of the conference, but the initial reading and discussion are conducted in as decontextualized a fashion as possible. In general, everyone knows the presenting teacher and what grade she teaches, so there are strong clues about the context of the work that cannot be hidden.

In every one of these workshops, the challenge of looking at children's work in this decontextualized manner was considered confusing, difficult, and frustrating. Liz questioned this practice a number of times. In the third session, she declared, "I find so much energy goes to figuring out who the child is and that feels very artificial. I mean, when do we ever read work without knowing who the child is?"

On this occasion, I responded, "Well, certainly, in your classroom, you always know who the child is. So why do I do that?" But then, instead of offering a direct answer, I asked another question: "Is there anything gained in *not knowing* the identity of the child when you first encounter the work?"

A bit later, Liz came back to this issue: "To me the essence of writing is to make an 'I am' statement. The person—and this came up last week— the person's voice and the energy in the writing are an 'I am' statement. And that's part of why some kids have trouble with writing, and then to totally deny the identity of the person. . . ."

This criticism seemed to me a rather harsh description of the protocol. I responded, "Well, the question, Liz, is that if the child is really present in the work, are we really denying them or are we just looking for them in a particular way within the work?"

Responding to this interchange, Annette offered her perspective: "I felt a lot like Liz, that a lot of valuable time was wasted because we didn't know the identity of the child because we were almost making up reasons for things that would be completely simplified if we just knew who it was. And yet, especially when I was choosing some of the other work, I was really glad that people wouldn't know who the child was because I really wanted to hear a real reaction to the writing and not to the personality of the child. I don't even know how to explain why, but some of the selections I picked, if people knew who the writer was, there would be a strong reaction because the children's personalities are so strong. But I think there are some really interesting pieces of writing there just to respond to. And it really does provide more objectivity and insight."

WITHHOLDING JUDGMENTS

In collaborative assessment conferences, teachers are asked explicitly to keep their opinions of the work to themselves. The structure leaves essentially no room for statements about personal taste (likes and dislikes), judgments of quality ("This was really good!"), or judgments of developmental level ("This is excellent for a kindergartner!"). As facilitator, I often chose to allow some judgmental statements, especially in the first conferences. I simply didn't want to cut people off as they did what is habitual: make quick judgments. As participants came to see reasons for withholding judgments in these conferences, I became more diligent in stopping people when they made judgmental comments.

This practice is wholly different from scoring sessions in which pieces or collections of student work are judged in relation to a set of criteria by teams of independent readers. True, scorings by independent readers are also largely decontextualized, although the prompt, or assignment, will be known to the scorer. Little information may be provided about the writer or the circumstance of the writing, but the purpose and premise of the reading are entirely different from the collaborative assessment conferences. In scoring sessions, readers are making judgments immediately and, in most cases, without benefit of conversation with other readers. They usually can, but are not required to, provide evidence from the texts for their judgments.

In collaborative assessment conferences, the purpose of the reading is to investigate the meaning of the writing and the child's intent (what the child was trying to say and do in the piece) to bring the reader closer to the child through becoming familiar with the text. This purpose presents difficulties for many participants. Meaning is subjective, and a teacher's grasp of a child's intent is speculative. Sometimes there is considerable evidence, and other times there is very little. In these sessions, teachers' concerns about the subjective nature of this practice were almost as constant as those about the decontextualized readings of the works.

These two aspects of the protocol—the decontextualized nature of our readings and the nonjudgmental character of the discussion—are based on a belief that seemed to be deeply unsettling for most of the teachers. Simply put, in relation to children's writing, there are no absolute or right answers about meaning or quality. Not only that, the structure of the conference demands more questions than answers. The structure encourages speculations based on evidence, and it requires thinking about how to teach writing based on reasonable but uncertain ideas about what children are working on and interested in.

To some people, finding a compelling question is a more important moment in the learning process than finding an answer. Although that belief is not at the heart of our educational system, it is at the heart of this collaborative assessment practice. This belief seemed to be quite disconcerting for many of the participants, but I also suspect that all the questions were deeply exciting to the teachers. Margaret was the most vocal about the delight she felt at times in this work. At the end of the final session, she spoke about how these meetings had "made me very humble." The repeated process of thinking she knew what was going on in a piece of work, and then hearing something surprising from one of her colleagues that made her rethink her whole interpretation, delighted her.

"[I would] think, 'well, this and this and this,' and somebody would come along and say something that would open up a whole new world for me," she said. She suggested that simply looking at a work with a colleague "and saying, 'What do you see?' and 'This is what I see!' [would be] immensely fruitful."

I came to understand that this kind of careful examination of "the actual work itself" can be a bit like stepping through Alice's looking glass. At first, the room seems familiar, but further exploration reveals remarkable surprises. Looking at students' work not only allowed us to see the child presented in a unique fashion, but also provided unique views of the classroom with its complex of materials, ideas, pedagogy, and approaches to writing.

QUESTIONS RAISED

Raising questions about the work did not seem especially difficult for the Gloucester teachers. In all the conferences, they raised at least a half dozen questions, and most conferences generated many more. At least three significant kinds of questions came up in these sessions. The first were questions that one could ask of any piece of student writing, and they concerned the context of the work (e.g., age and gender of the author and whether the child worked alone or received help). The second kind of questions were those that could only be asked of a particular piece of writing. They grew more directly out of the specific description of a particular piece.

The specificity of questions raised may well be an indication of the depth of engagement the readers have had with the text. The deeper the reading (which I take to be an indicator of the rigor and success of the descriptive process), the more text-specific the questions. In the discussion of "May Is," for example, participants asked many text-specific questions. One that intrigued a number of us had to do with why Jessica erased "thats the end" from the last line.

Further analysis of all the other questions that emerged in the course of the 10 conferences revealed that they fell into three major categories: teaching, curriculum, and assessment; the nature of writing in different genres; and children as writers. These categories are significant because they provide insight into both the participants' concerns and interests and what aspects of a child's work can and are likely to be explored through using the protocol. In working with numerous other groups of teachers and the protocol, I've found these categories to be consistently useful for parsing the questions raised. What I find significant about these categories is that they represent a range of concerns that cover many aspects of serious professional development in the realm of teaching writing. In other words, through collaborative assessment conferences, teachers are likely to articulate issues and concerns that are both important to them and significant to the field.

The first category encompasses questions about teaching, curriculum, and assessment. In the conversation about "May Is," for example, participants talked at length about the relationship between the lack of punctuation and the meaning communicated in the poem. This discussion gave rise to questions about when and how to approach the problem of teaching punctuation. Should Jessica's poem be corrected for punctuation? Can punctuation be discussed in the context of exploring what meaning Jessica wants to communicate? What could Pam do to help Jessica as a writer at this point? These kinds of questions may come up at any time in the conference, but they are most likely to emerge during the discussion of teaching moves. Other questions in this category explore the relationship between the assignment and what the child hands in. In particular, these questions address how children make sense of teachers' instructions and what kinds of assignments encourage creativity and expressiveness.

The second category is questions about writing in particular genres. Given the nature of the pieces we read, most of our questions centered around story writing, poetry, and writing with illustrations. Through the discussions of several poems, many questions emerged about the nature of poetry. What makes a poem a poem? Can a piece of writing be a poem simply because a child declares it to be a poem? These are obviously important questions, and although there may be no absolute answers to them, how deeply a teacher has considered them and their complexity will have significance for how the teacher structures an assignment and responds to students' writings.

The final category of questions raised in these sessions concerned children as writers and sought a developmental perspective. Here are three of the many questions I noted from the 10 conferences:

1. Do children imagine an audience when they are writing? If so, what audiences do they imagine? Peers? Teachers? Parents? Others?

2. How is a child's writing influenced by the things the child has read or has been read? Are those influences observable?

3. Is there a point in a young child's development as a writer when the child begins to desire standards, criteria, or rules for good writing?

Taken together, these kinds of questions represent a sample of sincere and genuine teacher concerns. If noted and pursued, they could easily provide the basis for compelling professional discourse.

WONDER (THE VERB)

There is an interesting paradox in considering the meaning of *wonder*. My dictionary offers two definitions of *wonder* as a verb:

1. a. To have a feeling of awe or admiration; marvel. b. To have a feeling of surprise.
2. To be filled with curiosity or doubt (*American Heritage*, 1993).

It is with both of these meanings in mind that I identify the act of wondering as a goal of participation in the protocol. Both have been discussed in this chapter. The poem itself inspired admiration, and we marveled at the complexity of the images and meanings in the text. We further admired Jessica's seriousness and playfulness as a writer and illustrator. Jessica's efforts reminded us of the challenge of becoming a writer. This is a goal we ask all our students to accept and embrace, but also one that takes years and enormous persistence to achieve.

We were also filled with surprise and doubt. Did Jessica intend this ambiguity? Were our own interpretations of the text reasonable? Why did others read this poem so differently from the way I read it? What, as a writing teacher, can I or should I do to help this child at this point in her development?

The combination of awe and doubt is a particularly potent mixture. Both have a way of opening us up to learning. We become engaged with the object of our awe, the text or the child or, usually, both. We become humble because of the complexity of the challenge of becoming a writer and the desire and seriousness of the child that leads the child to accept the challenge. We are also humbled by the uncertainty we feel as teachers, for we also face a remarkable challenge. We doubt our own capacities to meet the challenge, but we are inspired by our students.

The paradox I find in my dictionary's definition of *wonder* as a verb is that I believe "to wonder" is not always as passive as this definition suggests. Wondering is not simply being filled, and it is not always spontaneous or magical. Wondering can be an active effort, to "be filled." For example, we travel great distances to be filled with wonder in museums and in nature. We also seek wonder in the plant on the windowsill, and we find wonder among the children in the classroom. Wondering takes time, attention, and effort. It is not unlike prayer.

LIZ'S QUESTION—AGAIN

I left the last session of the Gloucester workshops with considerable uncertainty that Liz or I or the others had an answer to Liz's question. She wanted to know how her students, or any of the children in the school, would benefit from their teachers taking hours at a time to leave the classroom, sit in a room together, and talk about single pieces of student work. This question sat on my shoulder during the countless hours I've studied the transcripts of those sessions. I wanted to see if any clues to Liz's question could be found in what actually transpired during those sessions. In time, I found some clues.

Let's return to a piece of the conversation shared earlier in this chapter. Julie, Liz, and Margaret were reflecting about the conference for "May Is":

Julie: What I think is important about going back to the child and saying that "I've been thinking about your work" is the message that "You matter to me. And your work matters and you are on my mind and you exist in my mind when you are not with me."

Liz: "And I respect you. . . ."

Julie: "And I respect you enough to think about you or your problem or your work. . . ."

Margaret: That's why I think your immediate reaction may just be "Oh, that's very interesting." But if you come back with, "There are a lot of meanings here, and I wonder what you meant. . . ."

Liz: It shows you are really interested in their learning.

Why is this conversation so important? If teaching and learning are an interaction, surely the feelings between teacher and student will determine much about the success of that interaction. Arguably, respect is the critical feeling for a mutually beneficial relationship. But it cannot be respect built entirely on role or some other general quality ("authority figure" or "older person"). The stresses of classroom life are too great to sustain respect built on such an abstract foundation. Respect must rest solidly on the particulars of the specific people involved. Teacher and student must come to know, appreciate, and respect the passions, curiosities, experiences, efforts, and accomplishments of each other. This type of respect doesn't happen quickly. When it develops, it builds, I suspect, from genuine interest in each other as individuals. That interest has to come from some interaction that makes one take notice of another.

Talking about respecting children and their work seems easy. Many of us in education do this kind of talking all the time. I worry, though, that we often like the idea of respecting children more than we actually experience the feeling deeply enough to inform and guide our behavior. I worry because so much of what I've seen in schools—from the condition of buildings and learning materials to many of the daily interactions between adults and children—seems to disregard and disrespect the very seriousness of intent and complexity of thought that we saw demonstrated over and over in the 10 texts we examined. Real respect is not a simple thing to build. I suspect it rests best on particulars, and it sits poorly on generalities.

Over three months, these 10 teachers left their classrooms to sit around a table and read and discuss children's writing. In our 18 hours together in the superintendent's meeting room and the school library, our examinations of these texts followed the pattern established by the protocol. We started by looking, and we dwelled on what we saw. As we looked more, we saw more, and in turn, we became more interested. Interest kept us looking, and as even more was revealed to us, we became amazed. Through all this time, we deepened our appreciation of the complexity of the tasks undertaken by these children and the significance of their accomplishments. In short, we felt respect.

Our work made us want to meet these children, to get to know them, to ask them our questions and hear their answers, to tell them what confused us and delighted us and made us wonder. We wanted to learn from them and to help them in their learning. We wanted to look at the work of other children, too.

Much was unresolved when the last session was completed. Significant questions had been raised but not answered. Few of the teachers knew yet how this work would really influence their teaching. None knew if they would ever use the protocol again or sit with colleagues in similar sessions. Still, when we left the table at the end of our last session together, this looking and wonder and respect made a fine foundation, I thought, for going back into the classroom the next morning.

REFERENCES

American Heritage. (1993). New York: Dell Publishing Company.

Armstrong, M. (1992). Children's stories as literature: An interview with Michael Armstrong. *Bread Loaf News*, 5(1), 2–4.

Seidel, S. (1998). Learning from looking. In N. Lyons (Ed.), *With portfolio in hand: Validating the new teacher professionalism* (pp. 69–89). New York: Teachers College Press.

Smiley, J. (1991). *A thousand acres*. New York: Knopf.

REPORTING GROWTH

ARTHUR L. COSTA AND BENA KALLICK

Useful communication must always be in the language of the receiver.
Edward de Bono

W e are all familiar with report cards that assign letter or number grades for academic progress. But do you remember the days when report cards also included a grade for conduct? Schools have always deemed it important to report students' academic progress and how students conduct themselves as citizens of the school, but most schools never convey how students conduct themselves as *learners*. The habits of mind are an excellent framework for explicitly describing the behaviors expected of all learners. This chapter describes a variety of ways for reporting students' growth as learners.

Traditionally, parents, administrators, and members of the board of education are the most significant audiences for reporting. Teachers report to parents and to building-level administrators. Administrators report to the board of education. The board reports to the community. Many schools are expanding this concept of reporting to develop habits related to continuous improvement and learning. In these schools, students report to parents or board members. Parents report to teachers. Students, teachers, parents, administrators, board members, and community members all come to share a sense of responsibility for learning and accounting for progress.

REPORTING TO PARENTS

Because the main concern in reporting is communication, schools need to design reporting systems that are easily understood by those receiving the information. Although educators want to report everything they believe parents must know about a child's progress, good intentions and important information sometimes get lost in a fog of educational jargon. For that reason, parents should help design reporting systems.

Some design groups include parents; others rely on parent surveys, interviews, or focus groups. For example, Margo Montague, an educator in the Bellingham Public Schools in Bellingham, Washington, developed a report card through a process of teacher design, parent response, and final revisions. A committee of teachers developed a set of items they believed were significant to each child's cognitive development. With the help of a consultant, they presented these items to parent focus groups. The parents were asked to interpret the meaning of each item, and the focus group leader noted parents' confusion about any item. The teacher group revised the reporting process, using the focus group's comments as a basis. In the end, they arrived at a report card that had significant meaning for teachers and parents. (This process is described more fully in Chapter 6 of *Assessment in the Learning Organization* [Costa & Kallick, 1995].)

The John Lyman Elementary School in Middlefield, Connecticut, used a similar process to develop its report card. After careful consideration by teachers and parent groups, they developed a report card that uses the rubric shown in Figure 5.1.

FIGURE 5.1
Rubric for School Report Card

---

4 = Exemplary
  Initiates extensions independently.
  Reflects on own learning.
  Makes connections across disciplines.

3 = Proficient
  Works independently.
  Seeks help when needed.
  Applies acquired skills consistently.

2 = Developing
  Works on familiar tasks with growing independence.
  Begins to acquire repertoire of skills.

1 = Emerging
  Depends on adult or peer assistance.
  Has limited skills..

Source: John Lyman Elementary School, Middlefield, Connecticut.

Figure 5.2 is part of the Lyman school report card. This figure shows how teachers report data on 4th graders' growth in work habits, which are listed under habits of mind linked to citizenship. Lyman educators have also developed detailed rubrics that describe students' level of performance on these work habits. Figure 5.3 contains the 4th grade rubric for two of those habits: (1) makes appropriate choices to complete tasks and meet goals (persisting, managing impulsivity) and (2) shows thoroughness in work (striving for accuracy, thinking and communicating with clarity and precision).

At the Marcy Open School in Minneapolis, Minnesota, parents, teachers, and children consider progress in both academic subjects and the habits of mind. One page of the school's progress report lists each habit of mind with a brief description. Another area lists whether or not a habit was a "personal goal area" for the student that particular grading period. In another set of columns, the teacher indicates whether the student is using a habit rarely, developing it, or consistently applying it.

FIGURE 5.2

Excerpt from 4th Grade Report Card

Citizenship * Work Habits	Nov.	March	June
Makes appropriate choices to complete tasks and meet goals (seat choice, use of time).			
Shows thoroughness in work.			
Work is neat and legible.			
Makes smooth transitions.			
Takes responsibility for actions.			
Communicates needs, concerns, feelings, and opinions.			
Works cooperatively and productively with a variety of peers.			
Makes positive contributions to the school community (study buddy, school chores, school boards, senate, assembly).			

Source: John Lyman Elementary School, Middlefield, Connecticut.

Schools must also give parents the opportunity to report to teachers. In Nancy Skerritt's district in Tahoma, Washington, parents report to teachers about their child's progress. They describe specific examples of how their child is exhibiting the habits of mind at home. Another example of this combined reporting is from the Marcy Open School in Minneapolis, Minnesota. An excerpt of their report card is shown in Figure 5.4 (see p. 78). The school keeps the teacher report and the parent report side by side so that the child sees a paired comparison. In addition, the parent and teacher work with the student to set goals for the next quarter.

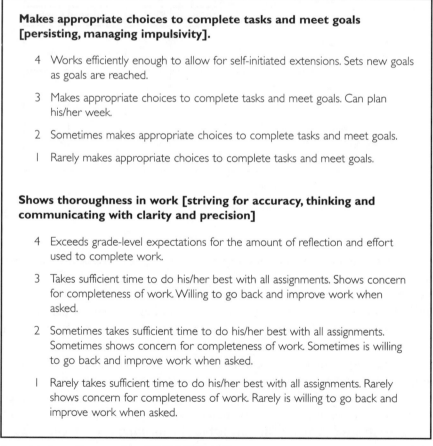

FIGURE 5.3
4th Grade Rubric for Two Work Habits

Work Habits for Citizenship

Makes appropriate choices to complete tasks and meet goals [persisting, managing impulsivity].

4 Works efficiently enough to allow for self-initiated extensions. Sets new goals as goals are reached.

3 Makes appropriate choices to complete tasks and meet goals. Can plan his/her week.

2 Sometimes makes appropriate choices to complete tasks and meet goals.

1 Rarely makes appropriate choices to complete tasks and meet goals.

Shows thoroughness in work [striving for accuracy, thinking and communicating with clarity and precision]

4 Exceeds grade-level expectations for the amount of reflection and effort used to complete work.

3 Takes sufficient time to do his/her best with all assignments. Shows concern for completeness of work. Willing to go back and improve work when asked.

2 Sometimes takes sufficient time to do his/her best with all assignments. Sometimes shows concern for completeness of work. Sometimes is willing to go back and improve work when asked.

1 Rarely takes sufficient time to do his/her best with all assignments. Rarely shows concern for completeness of work. Rarely is willing to go back and improve work when asked.

Source: John Lyman Elementary School, Middlefield, Connecticut.

Figure 5.4
Excerpt from School Report Card

Marcy Open School 20___

Student/Parent/Teacher

Progress Evaluation for _____ Grade: ____

Teacher: _____

Mark each behavior using N = Not Yet; D = Developing; O = Often

This year, I notice that _____ does the following:

	TEACHER		PARENT/CHILD	
	Winter	**Spring**	**Winter**	**Spring**
1. Keeps on trying; does not give up easily.				
2. Thinks out possibilities before answering a question.				
3. Listens to others with understanding and care.				

Source: Marcy Open School, Minneapolis, Minnesota.

PUTTING STUDENTS AT THE CENTER

Because students are at the center of all reporting, it makes sense that they should become a part of the reporting procedure. Many schools now are conscious of the need to help students learn how to self-evaluate, and they include students in the reporting process. Children are part of parent conferences, they write narratives for their parents on their report cards, and they grade themselves as a part of the report card.

Including students in a conference provides them with another rich opportunity to practice their habits of mind. They must be reflective and metacognitive, and they must check for accuracy and precision. As they organize their learning, they also make sense of their learning. They set goals for themselves that foster the habit of remaining open to continuous learning.

Teachers who work with student-led conferences usually write letters to parents offering them the option of attending the conference with their child or not. Most parents opt to attend the conference with the child. Sometimes, parents want a few minutes alone with the teacher, too. The teacher then offers activities to keep the student occupied during the private conversation.

At the elementary level, some teachers conduct four conferences simultaneously in the classroom. The teacher sets up such activities as

- Student shares portfolio.
- Student solves a problem that is on the board.
- Student describes the student's present work in the classroom.
- Student, parents, and teacher reflect on student's work and set goals for the next quarter of work.

The teacher is able to spend 15 minutes with students and their parents. Students are able to spend one hour with their parents.

Whatever the format, students prepare for these conferences in many different ways. In the Charlevoix-Emmet Intermediate School District in Petosky, Michigan, students use an organizer to reflect on their learning and prepare for the conference. They group their activities under three main headings: procedures and things to do before conference, procedures and things to do at conference, and a portfolio checklist. Other organizer sheets help students specifically summarize the academic objectives they worked on, the things they think they did well, and the things they want their parents to notice about their work. The organizer also offers a space for parents to write comments after they have seen the child's work.

WRITING NARRATIVES

In a classroom we visited in Scarsdale, New York, the teacher asks her students to write a narrative regarding their progress on their report card. The students describe their learning and how they might improve it. They also give specific examples of work in ways they have showed the most persistence. Throughout their description, they discuss how they use the habits of mind to discipline their work.

Narratives encourage students to be self-reflective before they see the commentary the teacher has made. This type of writing also provides an opportunity for students to measure their self-perception against the teacher's perception and, if there is a difference, talk about any misperceptions.

Sometimes, teachers write a narrative rather than simply report academic progress with a number or letter grade. Susan Martinez at John

Lyman Elementary School in Middlefield, Connecticut, wrote this progress report about a 2nd grader in her class:

Math Development

M— picks up new mathematical concepts quickly and is able to apply the new knowledge immediately to solve problems. She has been working on activities involving sorting, graphing, estimating (both quantity and volume) and place value. She has also been doing a lot of group problem solving. She is able to generate multiple solutions to a problem and can usually explain in words how she arrived at her solution. She is developing efficient strategies for doing mental computations. She enjoys a mathematical challenge and is willing to struggle with a problem when the answer is not immediately apparent.

REPORTING TO THE BOARD AND THE COMMUNITY

Schools must also report progress with the habits of mind to the school, the board of education, and the community. Although most communities consider the habits of mind to be important, they don't often take the time to reflect on the habits' meaning and notice improvement. If board members are already working on their own behavior—acting as role models for students and using the habits of mind to guide their work and communication—then they have a deeper appreciation for the assessments that are brought before them.

Many schools provide a profile of student progress with the habits of mind that are based on checklists and self-evaluation profiles. For example, the rubrics shown in Figures 3.3–3.7 (Chapter 3) can be used to track students over time. A graph will show progress and areas where students still need work.

Students can also make presentations reflecting their understanding of the habits. Through the preparation and presentation, they become living models of using the habits. Community events are an important opportunity for students to showcase how they use the habits of mind. They can participate in planning, implementing, and evaluating events.

For example, Back-to-School-Night is a prime event where students can show their understanding of the habits. Ask students to provide examples of their classroom work with the habits of mind. Students who are keeping electronic portfolios often have examples of their use of the habits as they work with a team to solve a problem. Parents, board members, and community representatives are thrilled to see actual video clips showing students thinking interdependently, listening with understanding and empathy, and questioning and posing problems.

Invite board members to hear students speak to parents about their study of the habits of mind. At Meadowview Elementary School in Eau Claire, Wisconsin, teams of 6th grade students used their public speaking skills to present the habits of mind to the city council. (City Council members commented that they became self-analytical about their own behaviors as a result!)

Although the habits of mind don't readily translate into numbers, they can easily be observed in the context of daily life. Board members will need to get used to trusting their own observations rather than looking for quantifiable measurements of the habits' success. Board members should be able to find examples of students' progress with the habits from students' employers, parents, and students themselves as they demonstrate the use of the habits in public occasions.

Eventually, educators, students, parents, and community members will begin to see the influence of the habits of mind in the community at large. For example, at Zelda's Restaurant in Adrian, Michigan, you'll find a large poster listing the habits of mind. The restaurant owner, impressed by the use of the habits of mind in the schools, decided to use the same list as a guide for her employees. Each week, the coworkers agree to focus on a particular habit, and they practice the behaviors as they serve customers. Children who eat in that restaurant are reinforced by the visible attention to the same behaviors they are learning in school.

PROMOTING SELF-EVALUATION

Ultimately, the most enduring legacy of evaluation is the habit of self-assessment. When students internalize a sense of what constitutes high-quality work, they will work toward that goal without prompting.

Ask students to assess their own work against carefully crafted rubrics that define different levels of performance. (See Chapter 3 for several sample rubrics.) Many teachers ask students to fill out a self-assessment survey a few times in the school year. Then, students create a graph of their progress (or lack of it!). They can use this information to report to their parents in a conference or as an addendum to their report card. Teachers can easily create a simple survey that asks students to rate their development of all the habits of mind on a continuum from "not using yet but I'm learning" to "I usually try to behave this way." Figure 5.5 (see p. 82)

Figure 5.5
Sample Rate Your Intelligent Behavior Statements

1. I am a persistent person. If I don't succeed on the first try, I keep trying until I do succeed.

2. I manage my impulses and am willing to delay gratification in order to attain long-term goals.

3. I listen to others with empathy and understanding.

4. I am a flexible thinker and seek new ways of looking at things.

5. I try to be aware of *how* I am thinking (metacognition) when I am trying new ways to solve a problem.

6. I check my work for quality and try to be accurate and precise no matter what I am doing.

Source: **Steve Huffman, Kalani High School, Honolulu, Hawaii.**

contains sample statements from a survey created by Steve Huffman at Kalani High School in Honolulu, Hawaii.

Another strategy is to ask students to complete a "self-report" for next year's teacher. Many teachers ask their students to write a letter to the teacher they'll have the following year. In Eau Claire, Wisconsin, students send to next year's teacher a description of themselves. Here is an excerpt from one student's work:

> I am a hands-on, auditory, and visual learner. But the two methods of learning I prefer to use the most are auditory and visual. When I do math, I like to have the problem in front of me so I can keep looking it over as many times as I want until I get the answer. . . . In social studies, I am an auditory learner. . . .
>
> When I work in class I like to work with a partner . . . because you get a chance to have two different opinions so you become flexible in your thinking. . . .
>
> When I work in a group, my strength is contributing a lot because I am not shy. That's why I think the habit of mind that I use the most is risk taking. My weakness when I work in groups is that I give in quickly in order to move on. The habit of mind that I would like to concentrate working on the most is metacognition because it lets you think about how you do things.

Don't forget the importance of celebrating students' achievements, too. Most schools have trophy cases for sports, and they offer a variety of honors and awards for high grades. Why not offer awards for students who exhibit the habits of mind? Waikiki Elementary School and Royal Elementary School in Honolulu, Hawaii, offer certificates for outstanding use of the habits of mind. There are myriad possibilities for celebrating students' achievement and signalling the community's belief that the habits of mind are worth striving for.

Reporting honors progress identifies areas for growth and celebrates the strengthening of the entire school community. A school will celebrate and reward what it values. As the habits of mind become valued, so too will their achievements be recognized.

REFERENCE

Costa, A., & Kallick, B. (1995). *Assessment in the learning organization: Shifting the paradigm*. Alexandria, VA: Association for Supervision and Curriculum Development.

In this powerful example from a 4th grade classroom, Steven Levy demonstrates how much discipline of mind it takes to accomplish a high-quality task. He focuses on habits of mind that call for striving for accuracy, thinking flexibly, persisting, and remaining open to continuous learning as he encourages his students to craft a set of lines, which serve as metaphor for crafting any sort of work.

—Arthur L. Costa and Bena Kallick

6

BUILDING A CULTURE WHERE HIGH QUALITY COUNTS

"Mr. Levy? Is this done?"
"Mr. Levy? Is this good?"
"Mr. Levy? How's this?"
The line of students stretches back from my chair, disappearing into the clumps of desks where other students finishing their work wait with fear and expectation for the verdict they inevitably must face. Somehow, the line never ends. It snakes on and on as convicted students tread a well-worn path from my throne of judgment to their seats of reluctant revision—until each is finally released with my coveted seal of approval.
"Yes, Natasha, it looks good."
"I like that, Joseph. Excellent work."
"Great, Marcia! Put it in your folder."

Note: An earlier version of this chapter appeared in the March 1999 issue of *Educational Leadership*: "The End of the Never-Ending Line" by Steven Levy, ([56]6: 74–77).

Sometimes students present work that demonstrates care and a striving for high quality, even if it has a long way to go before it is complete. More often, I am disheartened by the thoughtless, careless work that my students turn in and incredulous that they expect my approval.

"Are you kidding, John? Get back to work. This is so sloppy I can't even read it!"

"Have you read this yourself, Lisette? It doesn't make any sense. Please read it yourself before you show it to me."

"Is that all, Ross? You haven't even begun to describe what a pulley is, and your drawing is totally incomplete. Go back and read the directions."

Most teachers know the frustrations of trying to inspire students to produce high-quality work. We encourage and exhort, bribe and threaten, but somehow our efforts fail to yield the intended results. How can we equip our students to take more responsibility for their own work? How do we communicate that everything they do matters? How can we build a culture where high quality is the norm? In short, how do we get rid of those never-ending lines of students awaiting evaluation? It took me 25 years of teaching to consciously address the challenge of permeating the culture of my classroom with habits of thoughtfulness and care—of creating an "ethic of excellence" to inspire my students to strive for their best in every assignment they encounter.

WHAT IS WORK?

I've learned that if I really want to solve a problem in class, I need to involve the students. So I began the school year by asking my 4th graders to consider: "What is work? What do you need to do your best work?"

A lively discussion of what at first seemed obvious soon ran into the subtle complexities of defining *work*. For example, what is the difference between work and play? Some say, "Work is what you have to do. Play is what you like to do." Does that mean if you like what you are doing, it is not work? When a baseball player practices his craft, is that work or play? When a musician plays music, is that work or play? If I love writing, does that mean it's not work? Or on the other hand, if I have to play soccer in gym but don't like it, is that play or work?

After much provocative discussion, students began to describe what they needed to produce their best, whether it was work or play. They ended up with five provisions:

1. "We need to know what the assignment is. We have to be clear about what is expected." I translated this as *standards*.

2. "We need to see examples." I called this *models*.

3. "We need a chance to practice." *Practice* sounded good to me, too.

4. "We need someone to tell us if it's good or not." I called this *feedback*.

5. "We have to have time to do it over again." This is what we called *revision*.

"If we wanted to draw it," I asked, "what would this working process look like?" Questions like this help students use other senses to contribute to their understanding. They learn to make pictures of an idea and to interpret the idea in a picture. Again, after much discussion, we decided "work" should be a circle. The final revision step would bring us back to where we started: the standards. We called the resulting tool our Learning Wheel, and we painted a large poster of it, which we displayed in the front of the classroom (see Figure 6.1).

The Learning Wheel was a helpful tool in beginning to challenge students to reflect on their own work. When they got stuck and rushed to me for help, I was able to ask questions: "Where are you on the Learning Wheel? Do you need feedback, or do you need time to practice? Do you

FIGURE 6.1

Defining *Work*

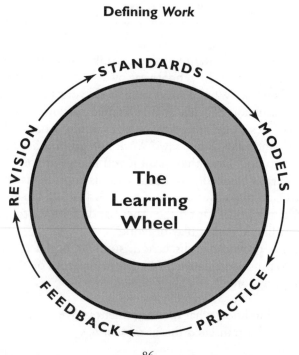

understand the standards? Do you need to see models?" Identifying their place on the Learning Wheel became a way for students to begin to take some responsibility for their own work. Instead of my telling them what to do, the wheel helped them define their own problem and articulate what they needed to make progress.

GETTING STUDENTS MORE INVOLVED

The Learning Wheel was a step in helping my students take more responsibility for their learning, but it did not significantly reduce that dreaded, never-ending line around my desk. The wheel also didn't do much to improve the quality of students' work. I still defined the standards, but defining clear standards did not ensure students would understand what the standards looked like or how to reach them. I was still responsible for showing models. Seeing models and being able to produce comparable work were two different things. I came to see that students would need skills and training to do the work well. I was still the only one whom they sought for feedback.

If I wanted students to take more responsibility for high-quality work, I clearly needed to get them more involved in every step of the process. Even if I did have some success in one assignment, that success would not necessarily carry over to the next. I needed to create a culture where everything they did counted. I could not fight the quality battle over and over again for every piece of work. I needed to establish the value that everything they do counts.

Establishing value is really what defines a classroom. We demonstrate what we care about by how we spend our time and attention. If I make time every day for us to talk about how we treat each other, my students know that our relationships are important. If I witness unkind deeds and ignore them, I communicate that kindness does not count. If I set high expectations and devote time and effort to their achievement, evaluate progress, and plan how to improve, students will develop the habit of striving for excellence. If I give assignment after assignment and accept work that is not their best, they develop the habit of applying just enough effort to get by.

Habits are built from the bricks of repetition. They are not something you get in one big block and call your own. They need to be practiced over and over until they become part of your nature. They are best mastered when introduced and practiced with elementary tasks and then applied to more complex ones. If I wanted to build habits that would lead to high-quality work, and thus establish a culture where high quality is the norm, I needed to begin with an accessible but demanding task that each of my students could accomplish but still have room for improvement. I chose a deceptively simple activity for the first few weeks of school.

DRAWING A STRAIGHT LINE

I gave students the challenge of drawing a straight line. Through this assignment, I introduced, practiced, and established standards of quality that would guide our work throughout the year. I also began to help students develop the habits of persistence, reflection, learning from past knowledge, and continuous improvement. I used the challenge of drawing a straight line, from the initial assignment to the final assessment, to help free me and my students from the never-ending line up to my desk.

Howard Gardner (1983) believes that the most important moment in a child's education is the crystallizing experience: when the child connects to something that engages curiosity and stimulates further exploration. Every product I ask my students to create begins with some kind of experience. When concepts are forged in experience, they are more likely to be remembered and understood (Levy, 1996).

In designing curriculum, I always consider what experiences the children have had that are miniature examples of the principle or concept I want them to understand. For example, if I am teaching 4th graders about explorers, I need to find the time in their own lives when they knew the terror and thrill of venturing into the unknown. If I am teaching subtraction to kindergartners, I might help them recall losing a mitten or a sock. If I am teaching 8th graders about the American Revolution, I need to get them in touch with the time they had to abide an authority that excluded them from participating in the decision-making process. I build the concept of a new idea on the foundation of their experience.

If they have not had any experiences that parallel the concept I want to teach, then I have to create one. If I am teaching about the American Revolution and I want my students to feel the injustice of being taxed without being represented, then perhaps I will begin taxing them for sharpening their pencils, going to recess, or getting a drink. They are better able to understand when their own passions are ignited and they can see the principle through the lens of their own experience.

Sometimes the experiences that generate assignments or projects are major events, and sometimes they are simple observations or challenges. I strive to be immensely simple in the first week of school; I tell my students to look around the room and to gaze out the window.

"You will notice," I tell them, "that everything you see is made up of some combination of straight lines and curves. "Do you realize," I entice, "if you learn to master the straight line and the curve, you will be able to draw anything you see?"

They are mildly intrigued. It seems logical. Something has caught their attention. The thought of being able to draw anything is motivating and, for a moment, seems a reachable goal. They are willing to explore the idea further.

"Now, who would like to try to make a straight line for us on the board?" I call on several students to come to the board and draw long straight lines. The class observes the lines, noticing the straight parts and the inevitable slants, bumps, or bends. We do the same with curves, making large C-shaped forms on the board. Again the class observes the round parts, the symmetry, and the places they seem flattened or stretched. I act as if the straightness or curve is the most important thing in the world because, at that moment, it is. I push them to attend to the finest detail. I communicate the value that everything they do in my class counts and will be observed and evaluated with the utmost rigor.

After the group demonstrations, I give each child a drawing challenge (see Figure 6.2 on p. 90). I don't give a lot of instructions at this point. I like to see what the students will do on their own. The directions are on the sheet and the students follow them, more or less. Each one completes the drawings, and I collect the work.

The work will vary greatly on this first assignment (see Figure 6.3 on p. 91). Some students will be very careful and precise. Others rush to finish as fast as they can. I choose several samples of student work, which each illustrate a criterion I am looking for. I conceal the students' names and either make copies or use the overhead projector to show them to the rest of the class.

As the students look at the examples of straight lines, I ask, "What do you like about this work?"

Someone will observe, "The lines are all evenly spaced."

"Great. *Even Spaces.*" I write that on a piece of chart paper and show the next drawing. "What do you like about this one?"

"The lines are all the same size."

"Excellent!" I respond, and write on the chart paper: *Same Size.* I show another piece of work: "How about this one?"

"The lines are really straight."

"Right." *Straight Lines* is added to the criteria list.

"So these are the things we are looking for in your drawings: even spaces, same size, and straight lines."

FIGURE 6.2
Freehand Drawing Assignment

Try making these drawings freehand. That means no help from rulers or compasses. Plan carefully. No erasing!

Straight Lines
Draw 10 straight lines, same size, evenly spaced. Do not intersect top or bottom.

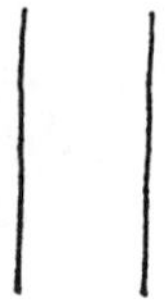

Curves
Draw 6 beautiful curves.

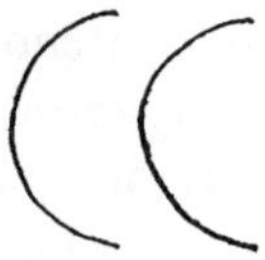

Diagonals
Draw 6 diagonal lines.

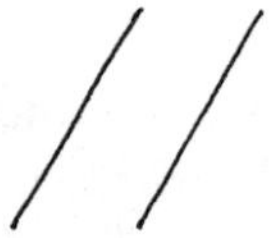

Circle
Draw a circle so the top touches the top line and the bottom touches the bottom line. Make it as round as possible.

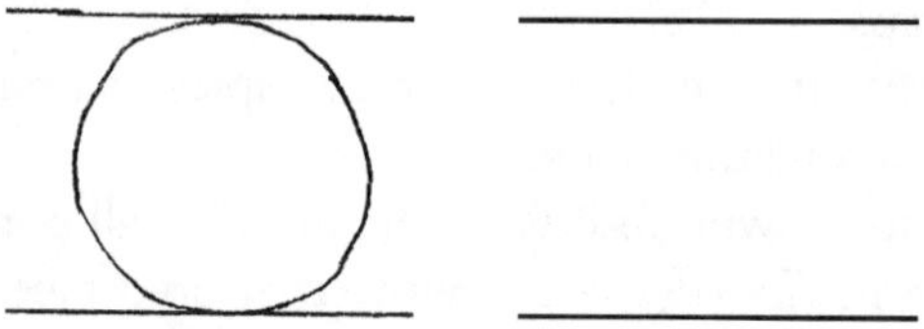

Mirror Writing
Write your first and last name on the line. Now make the mirror image below the line.

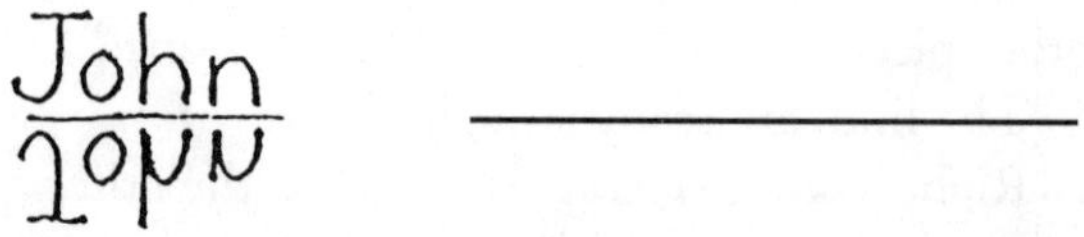

FIGURE 6.3

Student's Work for Freehand Drawing Assignment

Try making these drawings freehand. That means no help from rulers or compasses. Plan carefully. No erasing!

Straight Lines
Draw 10 straight lines, same size, evenly spaced. Do not intersect top or bottom.

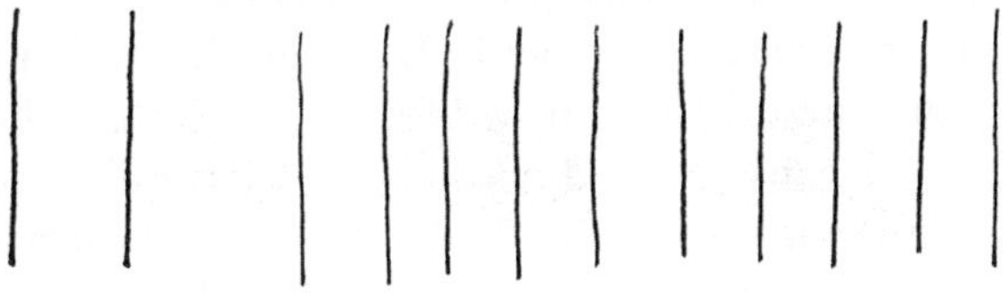

Curves
Draw 6 beautiful curves.

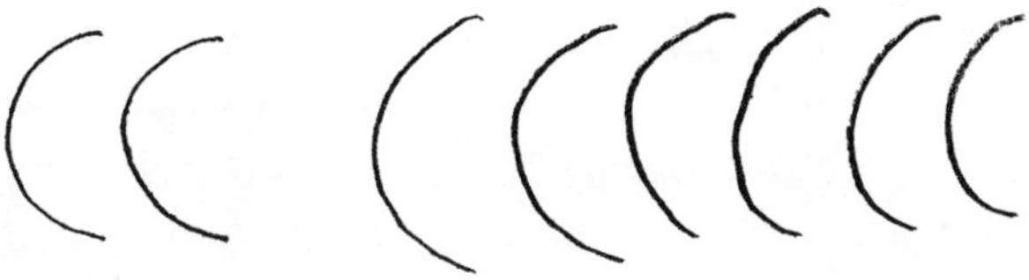

Diagonals
Draw 6 diagonal lines.

Circle
Draw a circle so the top touches the top line and the bottom touches the bottom line. Make it as round as possible.

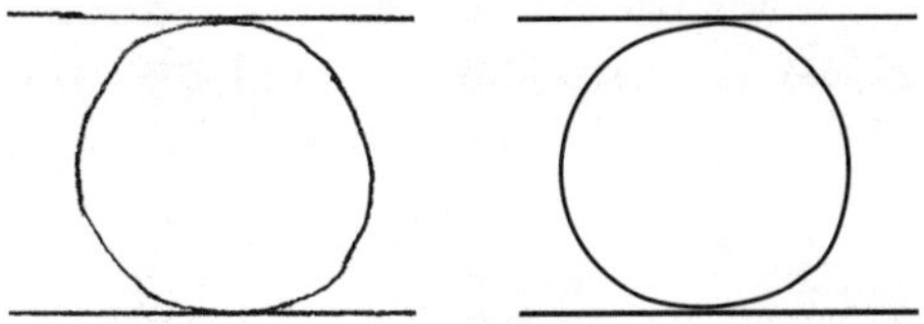

Mirror Writing
Write your first and last name on the line. Now make the mirror image below the line.

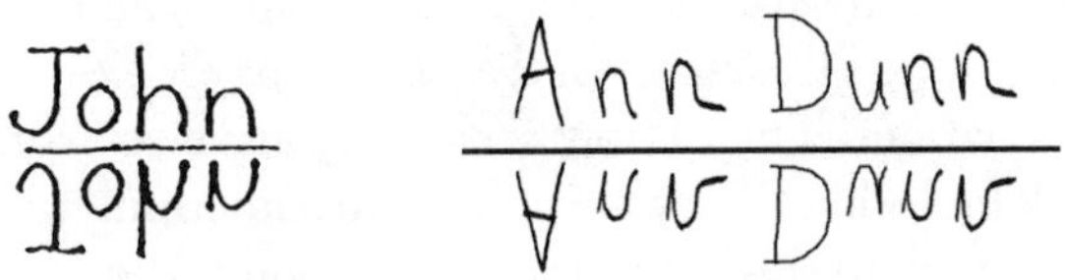

We go through the same process for the curves, diagonals, and circle. Identifying the criteria for excellence by looking at their own work gives students a clear understanding of the standards.

When I give them another sheet to complete, they are able to work with more focus and commitment because they understand what is expected. But the quality of the work still varies. At this point, we are ready to design a rubric to evaluate our drawings. I like to let my students experiment a bit before developing the rubric. If I define the rubric before they begin work, the students tend to follow the rules rather than think creatively about the assignment. Although the quality of their first effort may be inconsistent before the rubric is constructed, they often generate interesting ideas that expand my idea of what the assignment might look like. Only after we collect the first round of student work, look at it together, and establish criteria, do we develop a rubric to describe performance levels (see Figure 6.4).

The rubric provides written descriptions of performance levels. But if the students do not see examples of work at each level, they will not be able to evaluate their own effort with any objectivity. So the next step is looking at more work together as a group and evaluating a variety of drawings according to the rubric we designed. It would then become clear to them what a "1," "2," "3," or "4" looks like.

As we tried to evaluate our work, however, it soon became clear that our rubric had some problems. For example, if someone drew lines that were all very straight, but some were different sizes, should she get a "3" or a "4"? We needed to amend our rubric to provide a way to score each criterion independently.

Self-evaluation helps students establish a sense of responsibility for their own learning. It also increases their internalizing of the standards. The point of this whole process is to help students own the standards themselves. If you look back at Figure 6.2, the criteria were all listed on the directions the first time students received the assignment. But those criteria didn't really mean anything to them until they brought the standards into their consciousness and used them to guide their work. Figure 6.5 (see p. 94) shows how one student rated his work.

A rubric alone is not enough to enhance quality for most students. But when they use the rubric to evaluate their own work, they become aware of where it demonstrates the standards and where it falls short. They are better equipped to engage in the process of revision in a meaningful and effective manner. They know what they have to work on and what excellent work looks like. They are able to do something to improve their work without having to show it to me. At this point, the never-ending line to my desk begins to diminish, but it's not yet eliminated.

FIGURE 6.4
Rubric for Freehand Drawing

Name: _____ Date: _____

Straight Lines

	4	**3**	**2**	**1**	**Score**
Even Spaces	All lines are evenly spaced.	Most lines are evenly spaced.	Some lines are evenly spaced, some lines are close, and some are far apart.	There is little or no effort to space lines evenly.	☐
Same Size	All lines are the same size.	Most lines are the same size.	Some lines are the same size, some are tall, and some are short.	There is little or no effort to make lines the same size.	☐
Straightness	All lines are straight.	Most lines are straight.	Some lines are straight, some are curved, and some are bent or diagonal.	There is little or no effort to make the lines straight.	☐

Total ☐

Planning and Refining

4   I drew light lines first, then made them darker when I saw the straightness, spacing, and size.

3   I drew light lines first, then made them darker, but they were not all evenly spaced, the same size, or straight.

2   I drew dark lines first, then went over them to try to make them straight, evenly spaced, and the same size.

1   I drew dark lines first and did not go over them to improve them.

What I Can Do To Improve

☐ Plan more carefully before starting. Draw lightly at first!

☐ Work more carefully.

☐ Practice more.

☐ Other: _____

FIGURE 6.5
Student Self-Evaluation

Name: _____

Date of Drawing: _____

Number of Times Student Has Done the Drawing: _____

		Planning	Improvement
Straight Lines	1 2 ③ 4	1 2 ③ 4	1 2 ③ 4

Comments: I wasn't thinking and I put them too close together.

		Planning	Improvement
Curves	1 ② 3 4	1 ② 3 4	1 2 ③ 4

Comments: I rushed and put them way too close together, so they got messy.

		Planning	Improvement
Diagonals	1 2 ③ 4	1 2 ③ 4	1 2 ③ 4

Comments: I tried hard, but my pencil wouldn't make the lines go straight.

		Planning	Improvement
Circle	1 2 ③ 4	1 2 ③ 4	1 2 ③ 4

Comments: I messed up on my beginning (I pressed down too hard), and I messed up trying to fix it.

Mirror Writing
Comments: It was fun. I didn't do it perfectly, but it was very fun.

Notice that I have students evaluate not only the finished work but also the process of how they got there. I want them to become conscious about their planning. I noticed that many students in my class had the tendency to impulsively rush into the assignment, make mistakes, and ask for another sheet. At the other extreme, the perfectionists would keep erasing until the paper ripped. So I instituted a new challenge: no erasing! I taught them to draw very lightly the first time, and to look for the straightness, spacing, and size. Only then should they darken the lines. I encouraged them to go over the lines again and again if they weren't straight at first. I wanted them to experience the straightness in their hand, see it with their eye.

The process of planning is directly related to the quality of the product, so giving students time to reflect on their own planning strategies is important. Did they start lightly, or did they just make dark lines? Did they plan it out in their mind before they began, or did they just start drawing? I wanted them to reflect on these questions because if we establish a habit of planning, the quality of work is sure to improve. Planning how and where to draw a line begins to develop the habit of managing impulsivity. Students learn to control the impulse to race ahead and just get the work done.

I also wanted the students to make a commitment to improving each time they drew the forms. Some students have a tendency to draw the first lines neatly, and then get sloppy toward the end. I wanted the last line to be better than the first. I wanted each drawing they attempted to be better than the previous one. I wanted them to develop the habits of persisting and of applying what they learned from past experience to improve their next drafts. So I included a section in the self-evaluation for them to observe if their work was improving, inconsistent, or deteriorating as they practiced.

ENCOURAGING PEER CRITIQUES

More than anything else, peer critiques have helped me get rid of the never-ending line around my desk. Although I had done some work on peer critiques with my students, I first saw it used as a formal protocol in my friend Ron Berger's 6th grade class at the Shutesbury Elementary School in Shutesbury, Massachusetts. I adapted my rules for critique from what Berger does in his class. The critique has four steps:

1. *Say something positive.* This step creates a climate of support and col-

laboration. If students offer their work for critique, they know they are going to get some compliments.

2. *Observe something that could be improved.* The person giving feedback identifies some aspect of the work that could be developed further, in relation to the criteria that we have previously established together.

3. *Be specific.* Surprisingly, this step turns out to be the most important part of the process. Here is where I have to teach and intervene the most. Feedback must be specific to be useful. If you tell me my work is sloppy, I am not sure what you mean or how to go about making it better. If you tell me the last three lines are all slanting to the left, I can observe that and work on revising it. Here the question is always: What is the evidence? Describe the evidence you see to support what you are saying. They develop the habit of precision in language and thought.

Teaching students to give specific feedback helps further clarify the standards and develops a culture of effective collaboration. It also has a direct impact on the length of the never-ending line, because students begin to ask each other for feedback instead of relying entirely on me.

4. *Speak about the work, not the author.* I show students that we don't say, "You are careless," but instead say, "Every line from the third one on gets smaller." The work takes on an objectivity of its own. The lines are being evaluated, not the person.

After much modeling and practice critiquing as a whole class (we critiqued the critiques), the students are ready for critiquing sessions in pairs. Before they get into the never-ending line, they now have critique sessions with three other students. This method works because students know the standards, they know how to critique, and they can actually give each other helpful feedback.

Now that students have a clear idea of what is expected and what high-quality work looks like, they are ready to practice with a purpose. When they come to class in the morning, a sheet is on their desk. They take another home for homework. They apply what they have learned from previous drafts to each new attempt. They develop persistence as they practice over and over again ("Not again, Mr. Levy!") until they decide they are ready for their final evaluation.

They work on this drawing for about a week, during which time I manage to give each of them my feedback before they complete the final product. As I mentioned, they come to me only after they have had a critique session with three other students. My critique is the last one they endure before they complete their final drawing.

This will be the last time they do this particular drawing. They may ask to do their final work any time they feel they are ready (after having gone through all the steps above). Students are always scored according to the rubric they helped design. Because the students work at different paces and because they get tired of doing the same thing over and over, I have a series of drawings, gaining in complexity, for them to work on after they finish the first one (see Figure 6.6 on pp. 98–99).

I draw the first few forms, and students repeat them across the page. My ideas came from exercises the Waldorf Schools[1] call Form Drawings. The exercises begin with simple lines and become more and more complex as the students progress. These successive drawings provide a challenge and give students an opportunity to practice the strategies and processes that I am trying to establish as habits. There are a total of six drawings. Not all students master all six drawings, but students learn what it feels like to strive to do their best work. They practice the process of planning, reflection, revision, and how to give and receive feedback.

Most of all, students learn that they are in an environment where everything counts. I hear, "Mr. Levy, If you go crazy over drawing a straight line, what are you going to do when we have to do something important?" I let them shudder, imagining the worst! But if I can teach them to pursue high quality in the small things, they can use the habits they establish in more complex assignments. They apply past knowledge and skills to new tasks.

I always try to apply the skills we practice to produce an authentic product, a reason for the work that connects to something real in the students' lives. I know the exercises improved the students' handwriting and sense of form. But to provide a real application of their habits and skills, I taught them calligraphy. I am no calligrapher. In fact, I only had one lesson from a colleague, but it was enough to teach a basic alphabet to my students. They then used this alphabet to create beautiful, useful products like programs for our seasonal performances of music, poetry, and dance; signs and titles for displays and exhibitions; and historical documents such as the Declaration of Independence.

Calligraphy afforded some students a new means of expression. Consider George's writing and calligraphy in Figure 6.7 (see p. 101). At the beginning, his writing always looked like the words in the top part of the figure. And after all our line drawings, his writing still looked like that! As a matter of fact, his writing looked about the same at the end of the year. But look at George's calligraphy. Why is it so different? Is it that he cared about what he was doing? Is it that he enjoyed the beauty and was thus

---

[1]The Association of Waldorf Schools of North America is an association of independent schools using the pedagogical indications of Rudolf Steiner. For more information, please see http://www.awsna.org.

FIGURE 6.6
Student Drawing Assignment

Draw the forms across the page. I have drawn the first ones.

1

Draw a mirror image of the forms below.

2

Draw a mirror image.

3

Draw a mirror image of the forms below.

FIGURE 6.6—*continued*
Student Drawing Assignment

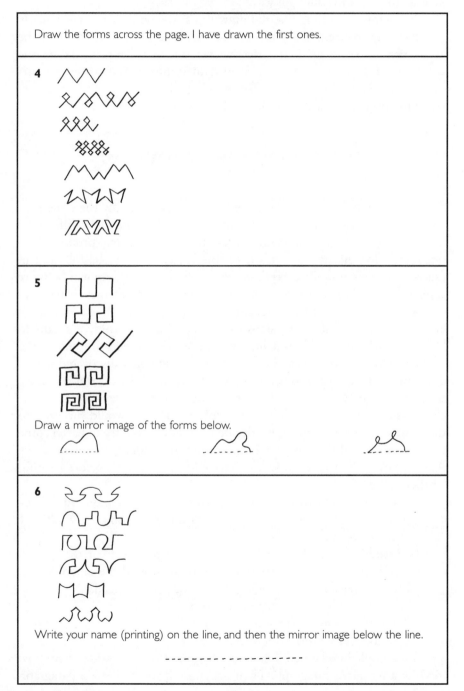

Draw the forms across the page. I have drawn the first ones.

4

5

Draw a mirror image of the forms below.

6

Write your name (printing) on the line, and then the mirror image below the line.

motivated to exert more effort? Did he begin to take responsibility for his own work? George became proficient in calligraphy and fast, too. Now he does all his work in calligraphy.

Practicing something like the drawings I've described is a particularly effective way to begin the year because everyone has equal access to the assignment. No one can do it perfectly; everyone is challenged. And no one is left out, because everyone can work and improve. When the students have experienced this process of producing high-quality work, they are ready to apply it to more complex tasks.

MOVING FROM DRAWING TO WRITING

After the line drawings are completed, we are able to apply the same procedure to produce high-quality work in writing. There are slight differences in the order of progression from the assignment to the final product. I do not intend for the steps described in the line exercises to be followed in exactly the same way for everything we do. Sometimes there will be more explicit instruction or direction at the beginning. Other times, I may recommend additional critique sessions or more practice of discrete skills between revision drafts. The steps outlined earlier are simply a means to help students produce high-quality work; they are not ends in themselves.

The writing assignment began when two students discovered a trap door under the carpet in our room. We managed to pry off the lid (using the principle of the lever, which we were studying in simple machines). The class was anxious to climb down and explore. I knew I would succumb to their excitement eventually, but I decided I might as well try to barter some work for the thrill they sought. I challenged the students to convince me that exploring the trap door would have educational value before I would let them climb down.

"How am I going to justify this to your parents?" I inquired. "They send you here to learn how to read and write and do arithmetic. What's the value of exploring a trap door?"

The students said they would measure the perimeter of the school. (The trap door led to a crawl space that went all around the school.)

"You don't have to crawl underground to do that," I said.

"We could study the heating system of the school."

"That's not in our curriculum," I replied.

"How about if we write about our experience?"

"It's a deal!" I exclaimed. I grabbed the opportunity to teach them how to write a narrative paragraph. Their assignment was to write a paragraph

FIGURE 6.7
George's Writing and Calligraphy

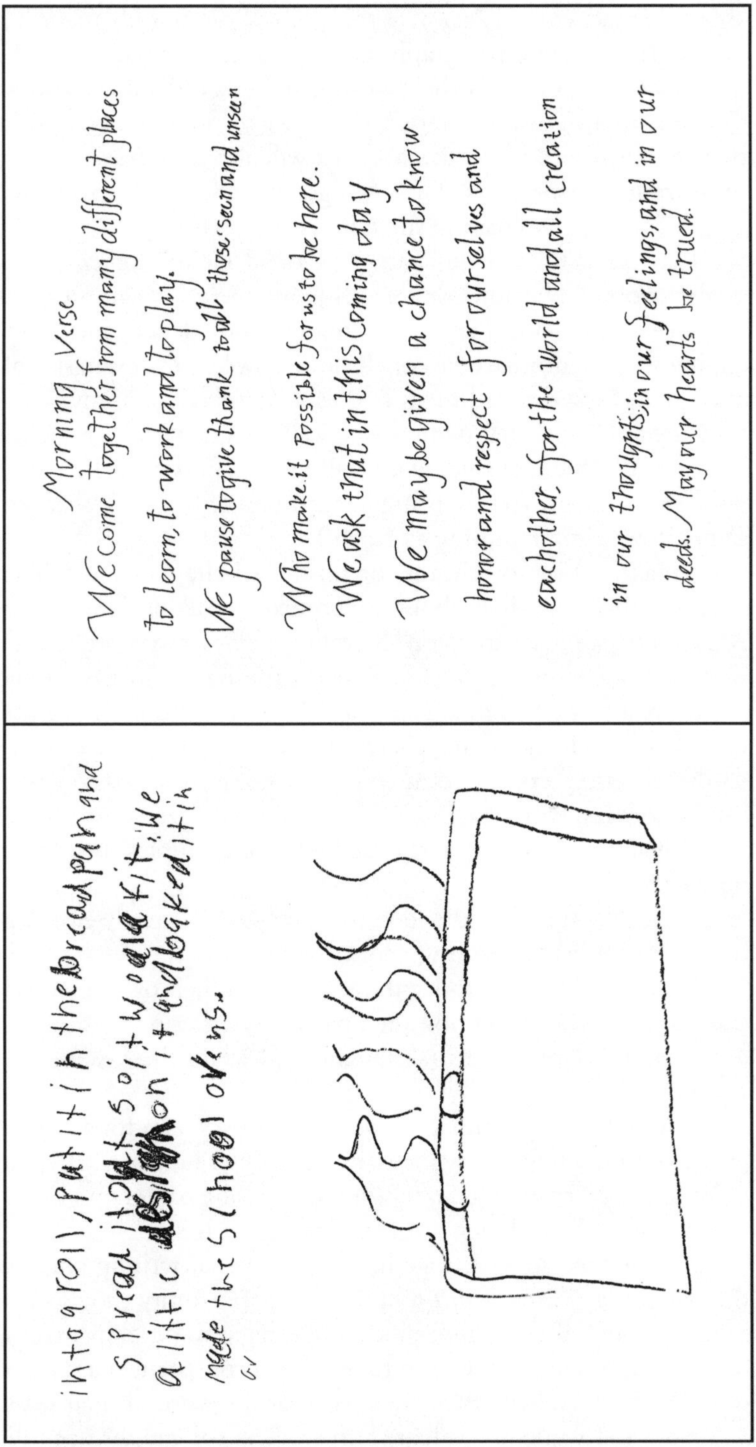

Morning Verse

We come together from many different places
to learn, to work and to play.
We pause to give thank to all those seen and unseen

Who make it possible for us to be here.
We ask that in this coming day
We may be given a chance to know
honor and respect for ourselves and
each other, for the world and all creation

in our thoughts, in our feelings, and in our
deeds. May our hearts be tried.

into a roll, put it in the bread pan and
spread it out so it would fit. We
a little dough on it and looked it in
made the school ovens.
G

about their adventure. Again, at this point, I did not offer much in the way of criteria for a good paragraph. Letting them write without explicit guidelines allows me to assess their writing skills as individuals and as a class. I discover important information about what kinds of instruction this particular class needs. Later, the students will also have baseline data to use in measuring their progress. They will get a chance to discover what makes a good paragraph by creating the criteria themselves.

I collected the student paragraphs and looked for examples of high-quality work. My standards for 4th grade include beginning with a topic sentence, supporting the topic sentence with details and examples, and ending with a summary or conclusion. I looked for examples of engaging topic sentences, detailed main bodies, and effective summaries. I may not find any one paper that demonstrates all the qualities I am looking for, but in a class of 25 or 30 students, I will usually find what I need. (If not, I'd write something myself or bring in examples of literature that represent the standard we are attempting to reach.)

I make copies, overheads, or posters of the work and have students observe what they like about it. Someone will notice, "I like the way Amanda began her paragraph. It really caught my attention and made me want to read more." I did not conceal the names of the students at this point because we had established a culture of collaboration in the class. It is good to reach the point where you can include the name—when standards, reflection, critique, and revision become expected components of all important class work.

"I really like the way Greg used a lot of examples. I really understood how he felt."

"I like the way David ended the paragraph. It really gave a good summary of what he was writing about."

If students did not notice these things on their own, I would ask questions to focus their attention on a particular criterion.

"Let's just look at the first sentence of each of these examples. What do you notice?"

Through these discussions, we define the criteria for an excellent paragraph and post it for everyone to see. We describe what makes an effective topic sentence, body, and conclusion of a strong paragraph. From these criteria we are able to design a rubric (see Figure 6.8).

Taking time to look together at samples of writing and discuss how they might be scored is important. This opportunity shows students what a "1," "2," or "3" really looks like. They begin to develop a common sense of what is expected. They need to develop a consistent standard before they can effectively evaluate their own work or the work of their classmates.

Now the students evaluated their own paragraphs according to the

FIGURE 6.8
Rubric for Paragraph Structure

3 **Topic sentence** has a clear, specific subject. It has a focus that lets the reader know what you are going to say about the subject.

   The body gives the reader all the information needed to understand the topic. It has descriptive details.

   The conclusion sums up the information or tells what it means.

2 **Topic sentence** has a vague or broad subject. It does not give a clear idea what the author will say about the subject.

   The body gives some but not all the information the reader needs to understand the topic. There are few descriptive details.

   The conclusion does not give a good summary or tell what it means. It does not directly relate to the topic sentence.

1 There is no **topic sentence**; the writer just begins describing the action or details.

   The body does not support the topic and gives little or no detail.

   There is no **conclusion**; the writer ends with no summary.

rubric we designed, and three other students critiqued their work. They did a second draft, incorporating the self-evaluation and feedback they received from the peer critiques. They have a better understanding of the standards at this point, so their revisions are focused and deliberate. I have them write reflection sheets that describe what they did to improve their second drafts.

Students still come to the never-ending line, but there isn't much of a line anymore. Everyone is engaged in different parts of the process, but more important, it all doesn't rotate around me. When it is time for students to show me their work, the quality inevitably surpasses what I used to see in the never-ending line. I look at their drafts, self-evaluations, peer critiques, and reflection sheets. Then I give them my feedback. Now they are ready for their final draft, which I will score according to the rubric.

We continue to write paragraphs and practice this process throughout the year. For example, we did a project on shoes, learning about economy and industrialization by exploring the countries where the shoes were made. I asked my class to find a shoe that had some character and a story to tell. Then I asked them to write a paragraph about it. I was conducting research about how drawing might affect the quality of their writing. They were asked to first write a paragraph about the shoe, then to draw it, and then to write a second draft. They did various reflections along the way, and they got critiques from classmates and from the teacher. Every student in the class discovered details in the drawing activity that enriched the second draft of the writing.

Finally, we apply these same steps to a long-range project. For example, last year we studied colonial life, and I asked students to create a fictitious colonial character for themselves. I challenged them to make the character so authentic that a public audience would be convinced that their character really existed. We began by discussing how anyone 300 years from now might know that you existed. Here is the discussion:

"They could ask people who knew me."
"Would anyone be alive who knew you?"
"Maybe I wrote something and signed it."
"Good. What kinds of things might you write?"
"A letter."
"A story."
"A diary."
"Great. What else?"
"They might see pictures of me or a video."
"Excellent."
"My birth certificate."
"My clothes which have my name in it."
"My grave stone."
"Now—how might we know that anyone existed in colonial times?"

They brainstormed a list of artifacts. We chose five essential artifacts that everyone had to create: a portrait, a physical description, three diary entries from three different times in their lives, a letter to relatives in their country of origin, and their epitaph. Each student was free to include any other artifacts they thought would help to prove their existence.

Students presented their artifacts to the class, and we established criteria and designed a rubric based on our discussions. They evaluated their own artifacts, critiqued with classmates, revised their work, and received feedback from the teacher. We also invited other 4th grade classes to our room to be an audience for a first round of presentations of our characters. We wanted to get some practice and feedback from fellow classes before we delivered our final presentations to the public.

For the final evaluation, we set up tables at a community event. Each student presented and defended her character before an audience of parents and community members, who used the rubric to evaluate the students' presentations.

I don't often hear, "Mr. Levy, is this done?"

Now they ask, "Mr. Levy, will you critique my work?"

"Have you had three sessions with peers?" I ask.

"Yes. I met with Rhonda, Dave, and Shana."

"What was helpful to you about their observations?"

"They liked the details I used in the body, but they said my conclusion did not really sum up the idea."

"Do you have your self-evaluation sheets?"

"Yes. Here they are."

"Show me what you have been doing to improve your work."

I have been able to vacate the "judgment seat" to the degree that my students have taken responsibility for their work and developed the habits associated with striving for excellence. When they apply these habits of mind and work to new challenges, they do not need to rely as much on me for feedback and support. I get to ask questions instead of render judgments. And no one misses that never-ending line.

REFERENCES

Gardner, H. (1983). *Frames of mind: The theory of multiple intelligences.* New York: BasicBooks.

Levy, S. (1996). *Starting from scratch: One classroom builds its own curriculum.* Portsmouth, NH: Heinemann.

This is an age of communication. We all expect to be informed, need to know how we are progressing, and want feedback on how to continue our learning journeys. Bongard and Lemmel describe an evolving set of communication strategies that help bring the habits of mind to light for all members of the school community. They especially focus on how to both inform and engage parents as critical role models and supporters of their child's development. The strategies are easy to understand and direct; the focus and commitment are deep.

—Arthur L. Costa and Bena Kallick

IMMERSING PARENTS AND STUDENTS IN THE HABITS OF MIND

JODI BONGARD AND JUDY LEMMEL

S everal years ago, the Tahoma School District in Maple Valley, Washington, conducted a community-wide project to determine learner outcomes. A committee of parents, educators, business people, and community members determined that for students to be successful in the Information Age, they must be able to work collaboratively, communicate effectively, and act as problem solvers. They need to develop strong interpersonal skills, be critical thinkers, and be quality producers, which requires them to be flexible, decisive, and self-directed learners. These outcomes are now the framework for helping Tahoma's students become productive members of tomorrow's world.

Once the district adopted the outcomes, we wanted to become intentional in teaching them (and the habits of mind behind them). We also wanted to make the learning meaningful to students and their parents. We identified three main focus areas:

• Teaching young students to identify and label their habits of mind and apply them in their learning.

• Modeling the behaviors in our own teaching and team collaboration.

• Communicating with parents to encourage their support as partners in the teaching and learning process.

This chapter describes the critical factors that have helped us become successful in teaching the learner outcomes and the related habits of mind. The resulting process has become ongoing practice in our learning communities. Our work has improved student motivation and learning, increased parent involvement and support, and refined instructional strategies.

INTEGRATING UNITS

We have both become active participants in writing integrated social studies and science units for the district. These units systematically present the instruction, practice, and application of designated learner outcomes, thinking skills, and habits of mind. We teach three comprehensive units a year over a three- to four-month period. Thinking processes and application of the habits of mind are taught in conjunction with core content. The habits of mind also become the foundation for developing classroom "Codes of Cooperation."

The district has developed three main strands that encompass the integrated units. For example, all K–6 students study units that fall under the umbrella of an America Strand during the first four months of school (i.e., Community Concepts, Early Americans, Puget Sound Communities, Washington State, Early American History, and Growth of a Nation). Two learner outcomes are emphasized during this time frame. As a result, every student in the school is focusing at the same time on becoming a community contributor and self-directed learner. The habits of mind that support these outcomes become the focused skills for teaching and learning the content. They also help establish a learning community within the classroom and the school as a whole.

We have written specific lessons for introducing, teaching, and applying habits of mind within the context of the integrated units. These lessons provide detailed instructional procedures for teachers to use as they incorporate the habits within the social studies and science units. They are available for teachers throughout the district to use as a road map (especially new teachers) or as a springboard for creating original ideas.

The habits of mind taught in our primary classrooms are directly related to the learner outcome on which we focus. We might begin with the behavior of attending (managing impulsivity), which is essential in developing a classroom community. Risk taking and inquisitiveness are also taught early in the year, because students need to develop these behaviors to become community contributors and motivated learners.

Assessing the habits of mind is an ongoing part of our integrated units. Students have opportunities to reflect on their application of the related skills as they complete unit work and relate to others in the classroom. Teachers use checklists and inventories to pre- and post-assess students' growth in each focused behavior.

Ongoing communication with parents is an essential part of our unit instruction. We send weekly newsletters that explain or list the habit of mind emphasized during the week. A parents-only Curriculum Night provides an opportunity for us to explain how and why the habits of mind are an essential part of teaching and learning in our classroom communities. Students share evidence of how they practice the behaviors at Open House and Portfolio Nights. Assessment tools that show growth over time are shared at individual conferences.

CUING THE HABITS VISUALLY

Bongard, who is also a technology support teacher, developed a set of classroom charts that include a graphic of what each learner outcome looks like. The graphic also lists the habits of mind and related skills as indicators. The large, colorful charts are posted in the classroom for ongoing reference. The posters provide connections for young students, showing what each learner outcome represents. The visual cues also help nonreading students construct meaning. We have found that children learn more effectively when they have visual cues to help them make connections.

Bongard also made smaller versions of the posters with graphics on 4-inch by 5-inch slips of paper to hand to students. When we see a child demonstrating a habit of mind, we give the child a positive behavior slip. As students collect the slips, they become familiar with the labels and indicators. The graphic representation on the slips helps students more easily identify each focused outcome. Figure 7.1 shows two sample slips.

The positive behavior slips label the habits of mind and the skills that support each outcome. The labeling helps us remember to state specifically the behavior the student exhibits that makes the student a complex thinker or a self-directed learner. The slips provide a way for us to be intentional in how we teach the habits of mind. We give out positive behavior slips many

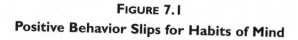

FIGURE 7.1
Positive Behavior Slips for Habits of Mind

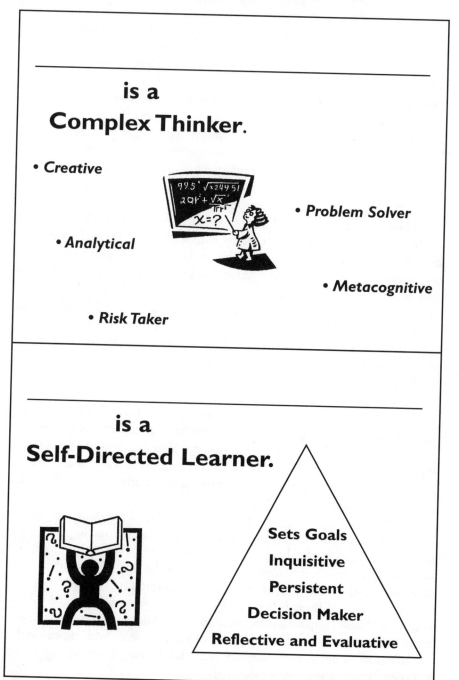

times each day. We intentionally reinforce and label both the outcomes and thinking behaviors. Because the indicators are listed on the slips, the slips help both teachers and parents see and learn the outcomes and related behaviors. Students keep the slips in the pocket of a desktop folder, so we can easily see which students need encouragement in practicing the habits of mind.

Positive behavior slips were so successful that before we realized what was happening, the system became a more intentional classroom management program. Desktop charts that reinforce the application of the habits of mind (and remind students when they do not apply them) have become effective tools for weekly communication with parents about student behavior. The charts provide an ongoing method for documenting successful application of the habits of mind. They also help us determine times when individual students are having difficulties managing their behavior. Figure 7.2 shows how a chart can be arranged.

The charts remind us to reinforce and label positive behavior each hour of the day. Students mark their charts with a plus sign for each hour they demonstrate the targeted habit of mind successfully. Each plus transfers to one minute of free choice activity time. Students can earn a total of 35 minutes of free choice in one week. Choice times provide students with the opportunity to engage in self-directed learning activities where they practice habits of mind (e.g., persisting; creating, imagining, innovating; taking responsible risks). Students who need reminders about appropriate behavioral choices black out the square for the hour they are not demonstrating the targeted behaviors. Each blackout represents a lost minute of weekly free choice time.

Concentrating on a specific list of indicators is much simpler for young students than managing a long list of behavioral expectations. The language is consistent in both the cognitive and affective dimensions of learning. The charts are excellent tools for helping students self-evaluate and set goals for improved performance. Behaving intelligently becomes the focus, rather than a student's lack of success.

As the years have progressed, we have included the language of the learner outcomes in our classroom Codes of Cooperation. Repeating the terms and defining the language as it applies in a variety of situations increase student understanding and practice of the skills. For example, one classroom code states: (1) Help the community! (2) Work together! (3) Think first! (4) Be self-directed! (5) Communicate with others! (6) Do your best! These simple statements reflect the children's terms for the district's learner outcomes. During a school year, students add indicators for the habits of mind in each category (e.g., Take a risk! Keep trying! Listen to others! Think about your thinking!).

FIGURE 7.2
Chart for Habits of Mind Behaviors

Collaborative Worker

1. Shares.
2. Shows empathy and respect.
3. Listens actively.
4. Is flexible.
5. Encourages others.

Name: _____   Date: _____

Time	Monday	Tuesday	Wednesday	Thursday	Friday
9:00 a.m.					
10:00 a.m.					
11:00 a.m.					
12:00 noon					
1:00 p.m.					
2:00 p.m.					
3:00 p.m.					

IMMERSING STUDENTS IN THE HABITS OF MIND

As mentioned earlier, two learner outcomes are taught with each integrated unit. We focus on each outcome for six to eight weeks during the year. As each outcome is introduced, we begin at the basic level so the children have a foundation on which to build. We read the outcome and habits of mind aloud together, and we define them using "kid language." Then we brainstorm what the outcome looks like, what it sounds like, and what it feels like. We remind the children of things they do that serve as examples of the outcome or behavior. For example, Bethany used precision when she cut out the pattern block shapes. She was a high-quality producer. We also share things that we do as teachers that demonstrate the desired outcome and behavior. For example, Mrs. Bongard was persistent when she helped every student edit her story. She was a self-directed learner. Because we intensively and extensively teach one or two strategies at a time, students get plenty of time for practice and application.

During those six to eight weeks, students are continually immersed in the vocabulary and language of the habits of mind. Each time we pass out a positive behavior slip or refer to the classroom chart, the children hear the vocabulary again. We provide individually tailored feedback for each student. We label the behaviors they demonstrate over and over again. Numerous times each day, the children are immersed in the language. The behaviors are reinforced across the curriculum in every content area.

Parent communication again becomes a focus, because the habits of mind need to be reinforced at home for maximum student learning. Immersion cannot be limited to the classroom. Students need to be able to discuss the outcomes and habits of mind at home with their parents, which will enable them to make connections between what they learn at school and the world in which they live. Guiding children to share the language of the habits of mind at home is one way to help them share their learning with parents.

We often have students rehearse a phrase that labels a habit of mind as a homework assignment. For example, we might encourage the class to share a phrase with their parents by saying, "When your parents ask you what you did at school today, what can you tell them?" As students identify specific behaviors, they practice a group response such as, "I was a risk taker when I read my book aloud during four-corners reading." It doesn't take long for children to come up with their own ideas of how to share different ways they practiced the habits of mind at school. We receive many positive responses from parents about the language their students use as they label what they do at school each day.

MAKING THE HABITS MEANINGFUL

We currently teach 1st and 2nd grades. To make the outcomes and habits of mind meaningful to those young students, we need to make them aware that these are the behaviors and skills successful people practice. We use real-life examples and experiences whenever possible to help students understand how behaving intelligently connects to their personal lives. We discuss people we know who are successful and the behaviors they practiced to become successful. For example, when we read a series of books by a well-known author, we point out how many times a book might be submitted and rewritten before it is accepted by a publisher, which leads to a discussion about persistence. This approach provides a meaningful connection for the children.

Parent support is most effective when parents are able to become a living part of their children's education. During our Community Concepts integrated unit, we invite parents to come to class to share about their careers. This time creates an opportunity for children to make connections between practicing habits of mind in the classroom and the way their parents practice them in the real world.

We work with students to develop specific questions they might ask about how the outcomes and behaviors are important in adult jobs. We ask parents if their jobs require them to be community contributors or self-directed learners. The children might also ask them if they have to be persistent, flexible, precise, original, risk takers, or inquisitive. Parents have the opportunity to explain how the outcomes and behaviors are vital to their success in the workplace. They give real-life examples of how, why, where, and when they apply the outcomes and habits of mind in their jobs. They also emphasize how important it is for children to start developing these skills at school.

This event is one of the most meaningful experiences for students. They begin to see the connections between success in the workplace and the habits of mind. The activity also provides relevance and motivation for children in practicing and applying these skills in their learning community. Figure 7.3 (see p. 114) displays a variety of interview questions we've asked parents about their jobs.

MODELING THE HABITS

Art Costa frequently emphasizes the importance of modeling as the most basic form of teaching. He believes that students must see adults using the same habits of mind they are teaching. As teachers, we model the habits of mind and learner outcomes daily by thinking aloud. We frequently label our own behaviors when we exhibit one of the outcomes or habits of mind. Our efforts send a message to the children that we are working toward these outcomes, too. Our modeling also provides students with examples of what behaviors and outcomes look like, and illustrates that people use those behaviors and outcomes many times every day.

The parent career program also provides life-experience modeling of

FIGURE 7.3

Parent Interview Questions About Being "Community Contributors"

1. How do you contribute in your work community?

2. Are you a self-directed learner?

3. Which kinds of risks do you take in your work?

4. How often do you ask questions?

5. Do you have to be flexible in your job?

6. Do you come up with original ideas?

7. When do you have to be persistent?

8. Is it important to practice precision in your work?

the outcomes and habits of mind. We talk about how the parents who share in our classrooms are effective communicators. The students notice when the parents elaborate or add details to their presentations. We talk about how the parents are risk takers to speak in front of a class. The parents serve as powerful models of the outcomes and behaviors.

The children also serve as models for one another. As we reinforce students with the positive behavior slips, we always label the specific behavior they are modeling. Students become very motivated to serve as models. During the first months of school, 1st and 2nd grade students learn how to label their own habits of mind.

PROVIDING OPPORTUNITIES

Providing opportunities is a critical element in teaching toward the outcomes and habits of mind. If we tell students we value these behaviors, we need to make sure our classrooms are set up to promote and foster the development of these concepts. We must provide and orchestrate opportunities for students to acquire, apply, and demonstrate the thinking skills, habits of mind, and learner outcomes.

Collaborative learning opportunities are needed. Collaborative groups resemble how people work in the real world. Learning increases when students are jointly engaged in problem solving. Students will learn the appropriate habits of mind from each other through the social interaction of collaborative groups. Small groups also multiply the opportunities for students to take control of their own learning, which promotes self-directedness and decision-making skills.

Research opportunities must be provided, especially at the early stages of learning development. We give students a variety of opportunities to find information for themselves, using multiple resources. Projects lend themselves to applying a number of thinking skills and habits of mind and require goal-setting and decision-making skills. They allow children to demonstrate their originality, elaboration, and persistence in completing ongoing projects.

Parents can become important resources in helping students select projects of interest, persist in completing projects, and find additional resources that support learning. We feel it is our job to communicate to parents the importance of their role in helping their students become collaborative workers, critical thinkers, problem solvers, and decision makers. We have found that parents respond positively when we communicate specific ways they can help their children practice the habits of mind as the children complete portions of projects at home.

When we ask parents to help with projects at home, we often choose one particular behavior and outcome on which to center. For example, when students are asked to complete models of a regional Native American dwelling during the Early American unit, we target family collaboration as the outcome and originality—creating, imagining, innovating—as the habit of mind to demonstrate. This approach takes the focus off perfection and accuracy and creates an element of fun and creativity for the whole family. The results demonstrate a wide variety of creative and original styles. The children simply tell how they practiced collaboration and originality in creating their dwellings as they share their projects with the class.

ENCOURAGING PARENT COMMUNICATION AND PARTICIPATION

The key ingredient to the success of our teaching and learning has been to consistently encourage parent participation. We provide frequent, open communication about teaching and learning. We incorporate a variety of methods for communicating with parents, including phone calls, written notes, newsletters, classroom awards, meetings, and conferences. Assessment also falls under the category of parent communication.

WRITTEN COMMUNICATION

Every six to eight weeks, we send home note cards with the graphics and indicators from the outcome charts and positive behavior slips. Each time we teach one of the six learner outcomes, parents receive a note card telling them how their child is successfully applying the habits of mind we have been practicing.

When a child has collected 10 positive behavior slips, we send the slips home attached to an award celebrating the child's accomplishments. We make positive phone calls home, and we ask the school administrators to make positive phone calls to parents celebrating students who have reached their goals in practicing the habits of mind.

Weekly newsletters tell parents about the focused thinking behaviors for the week. Classroom and hallway displays share examples of student projects, and the displays label the habits of mind students applied in creating them.

CURRICULUM NIGHT

We have a Curriculum Night during the first few weeks of school, where we take time to explain the habits of mind on which we focus and how each of those behaviors might look in application. We share a list of suggestions for strengthening each of the habits at home, which is defined with achievable outcomes. Conferences are used to ask how each child applies the behaviors at home and how the parent might encourage growth. Parents usually come up with original ideas that we can then share with other parents experiencing similar challenges.

LOOPING

Our teachers and students remain in a continuous placement loop for two years. While one teacher teaches 1st grade, the other teaches 2nd. When the 1st grade teacher takes her students on to 2nd grade, the 2nd grade teacher loops back to pick up a new 1st grade class. This looping provides continuity for parent communication and lays the foundation for ongoing trust and support.

CONFERENCES

During the 1st grade year, we have much longer conferences (40–50 minutes) with each parent. The initial conference is an opportunity for us to interview parents about how their child learns and to discuss the role they will play in the child's education. We ask parents to fill out an assessment of their child's developmental level in each of the habits of mind, and then we take time to compare that assessment to our own assessment. We discuss the similarities and differences in the school and home setting. Parents provide an important base of information about how their children learn.

PORTFOLIOS

Portfolios include student reflections about students' progress with the habits of mind as well as examples of projects where the behaviors were applied. Students self-select many of the artifacts, but we also ensure work is included that represents both the habits of mind students apply successfully and those that reflect growth and challenge areas. Students share their portfolios at a Portfolio Night held at the end of each unit. We also use the portfolios to document students' learning during individual parent conferences. We provide two formal conferences each year, and we are available at any time for additional meetings.

CHECKLISTS

We use a reporting tool at conferences and at the end of the year that reflects our support of habits of mind as an essential part of student learning. This simple evaluation checklist includes the learning outcomes and related habits of mind, rather than sections on work habits, study habits, or classroom behavior. We find this to be a much more effective tool for communicating student growth over time in a developmentally appropriate manner. Parent responses to this form are consistently positive.

PARENT VOLUNTEERS

Parent volunteers are an essential element in our learning communities. Some parents come in for half a day each week, while others drop in when they are available. Some complete projects at home, and others attend school functions or field trips. We make a point of asking parents how they want to help in the classroom and then honor their requests. They are here to support students' learning, not run copies for the teacher. Parents are more invested, and thus more reliable, when they know they are an important part of the learning community.

Parents work with students in small groups or one-on-one in practicing the habits of mind (e.g., listening to shy students practice risk taking by reading aloud, helping students who give up easily to persist through encouragement, and teaching students how to elaborate in their writing). We positively reinforce our parents as team members, and we provide ongoing appreciation for their support through newsletter articles and small cards or homemade gifts.

*   *   *

We consider our parents to be our most important assets in facilitating and enhancing student learning. Effective parent communication provides the conduit for establishing a team approach in education. They become the essential ingredient in establishing continuity between home and school environments as we focus teaching and learning around the learner outcomes and the habits of mind.

8

GETTING STARTED

ARTHUR L. COSTA AND BENA KALLICK

A s we've observed from the start of this book, assessing the habits of mind first requires thinking about what you want to measure. Most educators feel overwhelmed when they consider assessing all the habits of mind at once, forgetting that no one uses all the habits all the time. It is true that habits of mind do cluster naturally. For example, we cannot listen with understanding and empathy without calling forth two other habits: thinking about thinking (metacognition) and thinking and communicating with clarity and precision. But this example illustrates that assessing for one habit will require looking at two or three additional habits at the most, not all 16. What one or two habits are the highest priority in your classroom? Identify them, and they will help you define which two or three habits you will assess first.

Teachers will want to teach—and assess—habits on the basis of their students' needs, the content being taught, the context of that content, and any priorities established by the whole staff. These priorities will change, of course. When you work on a science experiment with students, you may want to focus on questioning and posing problems, gathering data through all senses, and striving for accuracy. As you reflect on the success of a project with your class, you may want to focus on thinking about thinking (metacognition) and remaining open to continuous learning. When you are working on a problem-solving task in a faculty meeting, you may want to focus on the habits of listening with understanding and empathy and thinking flexibly.

The following suggestions are intended simply to get you started with assessing the habits of mind. We provide many rich examples of teachers' assessments at the classroom, department, and grade levels and within the whole school. Assessment can begin at the classroom, building, or community level. Whatever assessments you choose, keep parents and community members informed about the need for the habits of mind and the improvements you're seeing as a result of your instruction.

Encouraging Self-Evaluation

If a school's ultimate goal is to ensure that students leave as self-directed learners, then the application, effectiveness, and self-evaluation of the habits of mind are significant. Promoting self-directed learning may represent a shift in thinking about the roles and identities of the teacher and student, so teachers will also want to assess themselves as they change.

One way to get started in this direction is to provide faculty members with a chart where they can detail the shift toward the role of "facilitator of self-assessment" (Hansen, 1998). As seen in Figure 8.1, such a chart can show faculty members where they began and where they are now in their efforts.

Figure 8.1
Self-Assessment Chart

Moving from ...	Moving to ...
Tacit expectations that are not understood by all students.	Developing a language of description so students can envision, see examples of, and implement their own work with a mental model in sight.
No time for reflection.	Creating time for reflection and self-evaluation.
Undervalued self-evaluation.	Overtly valuing self-evaluation.
No reporting to students or parents about the importance of and students' learnings about habits of mind.	Observing what is learned and what is not. Informing individual students, the whole class, the school, parents, and the public about progress.

When introducing self-assessment to students, the following guidelines are helpful (Davis, Cameron, Politano, & Gregory, 1994):

1. Discuss with students the purpose of collecting assessment data.
2. Set aside class time for students to make selections from the work they have produced, which is based on one or more of the habits of mind.

3. Work with students to establish criteria for their selections. Talk to students about the audiences that will see their collections of work (e.g., parents, other teachers, and community members), and determine the most useful way to display their work.

4. Include a feedback sheet that invites those who look at the student's collection of work to respond.

Sandra Parks and Howard Black (1999) have designed a valuable planning log to help students become aware of and apply certain thinking skills and habits of mind in their work. Students are invited to consider, "How do I learn well?" The list of questions Parks and Black have developed walks a student through the habit of thinking about thinking. They also have a specific reminder to students about how one can practice listening with understanding and empathy. The intent is for students to stay focused on a habit of mind for a three-week period. Students are invited to preview their work each week, stating their personal learning goals alongside the list of activities and assignments they must manage.

In a "How I Did" section, students are invited to keep records of important ideas they have learned, questions they have asked, feelings they have about what they are learning, and ways they can use what they are learning. They practice remaining open to continuous learning. Students are encouraged to keep work samples, journal comments, and reflections on their learning. The planner can help students prepare for a conference with their parents and teacher.

BUILDING RUBRICS FOR STUDENTS AND STAFF

Rubrics are a powerful tool for assessing the habits of mind. Create rubrics with students. Ask them to think about indicators showing their growth in the habits of mind: "How would we know you were using the habits? What would it look like if you used a particular habit? What would we hear you saying?"

You might want to create rubrics as a department. How can you observe students using the habits of mind? What would the conversation in department meetings sound like if all members of the department focused on habits of mind? What might curriculum planning be like?

Whole schools can create rubrics, too. What might a school be like if students and staff were just beginning to implement habits of mind (the novice school)? What might a school be like if it were transforming itself into a school that is a "home for the mind" (the transitional school)? What might a school look like if students and staff have spent several years successfully implementing the habits of mind (the school that is a "home for the mind")?

The chart in Figure 8.2 might serve as the basis for a rubric in your classroom or school. In each empty space of the chart, fill in what you would look for as evidence that your class was moving in the direction of implementing the habits of mind at each level. For example, what would a novice school look for when staff members implemented the habits of mind in instruction? What would a transforming school look for in instruction when staff members and students implemented the habits of mind? What would assessment for the habits of mind look like in a school that is a home for the mind?

Figure 8.2
Sample Rubric Chart

Level	D o m a i n s			
	Curriculum	Instruction	Assessment	School Culture
The School that is a "Home for the Mind"				
The Transforming School				
The Novice School				

Creating Study Groups

You might consider creating study groups to reflect on student work. For example, use the protocol described in Chapter 4 as a facilitating structure for such a group. Bring examples of student work to the table, and ask your colleagues questions like these:

• Do we see evidence of the student using any or all of the habits of mind?

• Where do we see such evidence?

• What can we learn about students acquiring the habits from their voice in their work?

• How are they getting better at the habits of mind over time as they matriculate through the school?

• How is this improvement reflected in their work?

Another study group tool is to post a large matrix in the teacher's lounge. Down one side print the teachers' names. Across the top, print the habits of mind. Hang a felt-tip marker by a string next to the chart. As teachers touch on one or more of the habits of mind, they should place a check mark in that square. Periodically hold a discussion in the teacher's lounge about who is doing what and how students are responding. What evidence is being gathered and by whom? Which habits of mind are being overemphasized, and which are not receiving enough attention? Discuss ways more habits of mind can be explored. Observe the chart for sequence: Is there continuity, support, and reinforcement across grade levels and subject matter? How can the sequence be improved?

Observing the Habits

As an individual teacher or in a group, observe students' behaviors and start to collect anecdotes that suggest students are using the habits of mind. Notice the context in which students are most likely to use the habits, and use this information to jump-start data collection.

Student observations are also instructive. Teri Ushijima, a 5th grade teacher at Mililani Mauka School in Honolulu, Hawaii, collected the following "Life Lessons Learned in 5th Grade" from students at the end of one year of teaching the habits of mind:

> This year I learned your actions speak more than words.
>
> It is important that you do your homework and school work accurately.
>
> I learned that if you think you can do something, you can, but if you don't, you cannot.
>
> It is important to learn from your mistakes so you don't do that again.
>
> I learned about attentive listening. You can learn more about what is happening.
>
> I learned that you need to control your impulsivity.
>
> I learned that you have to get along with others and work in groups.
>
> I learned to always have flexibility in thinking.
>
> I learned that perfect practice makes perfect.

KEEPING PARENTS AND COMMUNITY INFORMED

Initiate a study group to report student growth of the habits of mind to parents. Develop newsletters to inform parents and the community about the habits of mind and how they are important to the students' futures.

Design a report card or parent conference form that reports growth in the habits of mind. Explain the habits of mind at a PTO meeting. Also, describe how parents and staff can work together to collect evidence of growth in the habits of mind. Have students present the habits of mind to the board of education, the city council, the school site council, or various business groups and professional organizations in the community. For example, students can develop a videotape presentation describing what the habits of mind look and sound like in various content areas, on the school grounds, at work, and at home.

We must change schools so that they foster curious, self-directed, life-long learners. Although much education rhetoric states this goal, educators' behaviors often don't support it. The habits of mind are a language and core for changing behaviors.

You will find that once you begin to collect and assess the habits of mind, you will become much sharper about their meaning, their implications, and their use (Costa & Kallick, 1995). Useful data, thoughtfully collected, energize learning and practice!

REFERENCES

Costa, A., & Kallick, B. (1995). *Assessment in the learning organization: Shifting the paradigm*. Alexandria, VA: Association for Supervision and Curriculum Development.

Davis, A., Cameron, C., Politano, C., & Gregory, K. (1994). *Together is better: Collaborative assessment, evaluation, and reporting*. Armadale, Australia: Eleanor Curtin Publishing.

Hansen, J. (1998). *When learners evaluate*. Portsmouth, NH: Heinemann.

Parks, S., & Black, H. (1999). *Organizing my learning*. Pacific Grove, CA: Critical Thinking Books and Software.

ACKNOWLEDGMENTS

We wish to express our appreciation to the many contributors to this series of books. The descriptions of their experiences, lessons, implementation strategies, vignettes, and artwork are what give meaning, expression, and practicality to the habits of mind. To them we are eternally grateful.

We wish to thank John O'Neil, Nancy Modrak, Julie Houtz, Margaret Oosterman, and other members of the ASCD editorial staff who encouraged and guided us throughout this project. Our gratitude is expressed to our editor, René Bahrenfuss, for her flexibility, her striving for accuracy, and her persistence. We are appreciative of the artistic talents of Georgia McDonald and other ASCD design staff for the habits of mind icons. Without their attention to detail, striving for perfection, and creative imagination, this series could not have come to fruition.

We also wish to thank our assistants, Kim Welborn and Carol Hunsicker, whose secretarial skills and computer wizardry behind the scenes kept us organized and in communication with each other and with all the authors.

We pay particular tribute to Bena's husband, Charles, and Art's wife, Nancy, who tolerated our time away from them. Their love, encouragement, and understanding provided the support base for our success.

Finally, we wish to acknowledge the many teachers, administrators, and parents in the numerous schools and communities throughout the United States and abroad who have adopted and implemented the habits of mind and have found them a meaningful way to organize learning. The future world will be a more thoughtful, compassionate, and cooperative place because of their dedication to cultivating the habits of mind in students and modeling them in their own behavior.

TEACHER, SCHOOL, AND DISTRICT ACKNOWLEDGMENTS

W e would like to thank the many teachers, schools, and districts throughout the United States who contributed to the writing of this book. Their combined efforts helped us develop a comprehensive presentation of the 16 habits of mind.

California
Michele Swanson
Sir Francis Drake High School
San Anselmo, California

Tamalpais Elementary School
Mill Valley, California

Connecticut
Susan Martinez
John Lyman Elementary School
Middlefield, Connecticut

Hawaii
Steve Huffman
Kalani High School
Honolulu, Hawaii

Waikiki Elementary School
Honolulu, Hawaii

Royal Elementary School
Honolulu, Hawaii

Teri Ushijima
Mililani Mauka School
Honolulu, Hawaii

Massachusetts
Ron Berger
Shutesbury Elementary School
Shutesbury, Massachusetts

Fuller Elementary School
Gloucester, Massachusetts

Michigan
Charlevoix-Emmet Intermediate
School District
Petosky, Michigan

Minnesota
Marcy Open School
Minneapolis, Minnesota

New York
Central Elementary School
Mamaroneck, New York

Croton Elementary School
Croton-on-Hudson, New York

Kathleen Reilly
Edgemont High School
Edgemont, New York

Mamaroneck Public Schools
Mamaroneck, New York

Southampton Public Schools
Southampton, New York

University Heights School
New York, New York

Washington
Margo Montague
Bellingham Public Schools
Bellingham, Washington

Tahoma School District
Maple Valley, Washington

Wisconsin
Meadowview Elementary School
Eau Claire, Wisconsin

INDEX

ABOUT THE AUTHORS

Arthur L. Costa is an emeritus professor of education at California State University, Sacramento, and codirector of the Institute for Intelligent Behavior in Cameron Park, California. He has been a classroom teacher, a curriculum consultant, and an assistant superintendent for instruction, as well as the director of educational programs for the National Aeronautics and Space Administration. He has made presentations and conducted workshops in all 50 states, as well as in Mexico, Central and South America, Canada, Australia, New Zealand, Africa, Europe, Asia, and the Islands of the South Pacific.

Costa has written numerous articles and books, including *Techniques for Teaching Thinking* (with Larry Lowery), *The School as a Home for the Mind*, and *Cognitive Coaching: A Foundation for Renaissance Schools* (with Robert Garmston). He is editor of *Developing Minds: A Resource Book for Teaching Thinking* and coeditor (with Rosemarie Liebmann) of the Process as Content Trilogy: *Envisioning Process as Content, Supporting the Spirit of Learning*, and *The Process-Centered School*.

Active in many professional organizations, Costa served as president of the California Association for Supervision and Curriculum Development and as national president of the Association for Supervision and Curriculum Development, 1988–89. Costa can be reached at Search Models Unlimited, P.O. Box 362, Davis, CA 95617-0362; phone/fax: 530-756-7872; e-mail: artcosta@aol.com.

Bena Kallick is a private consultant providing services to school districts, state departments of education, professional organizations, and public agencies throughout the United States and internationally. Kallick received her doctorate in educational evaluation at Union Graduate School. Her areas of focus include group dynamics, creative and critical thinking, and alternative assessment strategies in the classroom. Her written work includes *Literature to Think About* (a whole language curriculum published with Weston Woods Studios), *Changing Schools into Communities for Thinking*, and *Assessment in the Learning Organization* (coauthored with Arthur Costa).

Formerly a teachers' center director, Kallick also created a children's museum based on problem solving and invention. She was the coordinator of a high school alternative designed for at-risk students. She is cofounder of Technology Pathways, a company designed to provide easy-to-use software that helps integrate and make sense of data from curriculum, instruction, and assessment. Kallick's teaching appointments have included Yale University School of Organization and Management, University of Massachusetts Center for Creative and Critical Thinking, and Union Graduate School. She was previously on the board of the Apple Foundation and is presently on the board of Jobs for the Future. Kallick can be reached at 12 Crooked Mile Rd., Westport, CT 06880; phone/fax: 203-227-7261; e-mail: bkallick@aol.com.

Jodi Bongard is currently dean of students at Lake Wilderness Elementary School in the Tahoma School District in Maple Valley, Washington. Before becoming dean, she was a 1st and 2nd grade continuous improvement placement teacher. She has been a collaborative author of the district's primary integrated curriculum notebooks, which incorporate thinking skills and intelligent behaviors through process-based learning. Throughout the state, Bongard has taught numerous workshops designed to help teachers integrate the habits of mind into their curriculum. She also served as the technology resource teacher for her building. Bongard can be reached at 24216 Witte Rd., SE, Maple Valley, WA 98038; phone: 425-432-4404; e-mail: jbongard@tahoma.wednet.edu.

Judy Lemmel teaches 1st and 2nd grade continuous placement in the Tahoma School District in Maple Valley, Washington. She has been the primary editor of the district's integrated curriculum notebooks, which incorporate thinking skills and the habits of mind through process-based learning. Lemmel teaches in the Masters in Education Program for City University in Renton, Washington. She is also the curriculum resource teacher for her elementary school. Lemmel can be reached at 24216 Witte Rd., SE, Maple Valley, WA 98038; phone: 425-432-4404; e-mail: jlemmel@tahoma.wednet.edu.

Steven Levy is a teacher and consultant who currently splits his time between teaching his 4th grade class at the Bowman School in Lexington,

Massachusetts, and consulting for Expeditionary Learning/Outward Bound. In his 25-year teaching career, he has taught every grade level from kindergarten through college. He was recognized as the 1992–93 Massachusetts Teacher of the Year, and he was honored as the Outstanding General Elementary Teacher by the Walt Disney Company in 1994–95. His book, *Starting from Scratch*, was published by Heinemann in 1996. Levy can be reached at 11 Fletcher Ave., Lexington, MA 02420; phone/fax: 781-862-9249; e-mail: levys@massed.net.

David Perkins, codirector of Harvard Project Zero, is a senior research associate at the Harvard Graduate School of Education. He is the author of several books, including *Smart Schools: From Training Memories to Educating Minds* and *Outsmarting IQ: The Emerging Science of Learnable Intelligence,* and many articles. He has helped develop instructional programs and approaches for teaching understanding and thinking, including initiatives in South Africa, Israel, and Latin America. He is a former Guggenheim Fellow. Perkins can be reached at Project Zero, Harvard Graduate School of Education, 323 Longfellow Hall, 13 Appian Way, Cambridge, MA 02138; phone: 617-495-4342; fax: 617-496-4288; e-mail: David_Perkins@pz.harvard.edu.

Steve Seidel is a lecturer on education at the Harvard Graduate School of Education and a research associate at Harvard Project Zero. At Project Zero, he is principal investigator for several projects that examine teachers' reflective practices, the close examination of student work, and documentation of learning. His work and writing for the past decade have largely focused on the collaborative assessment of student work. Before coming to Project Zero, he taught theater and language arts in Boston area high schools for 17 years. Seidel can be reached at Harvard Project Zero, University Place, 124 Mt. Auburn St., Cambridge, MA 02138; phone: 617-495-4342; fax: 617-495-9709; e-mail: steve_seidel@pz.harvard.edu.

ASCD stock numbers are in parentheses.

Audiotapes
Connecting the Curriculum: Using an Integrated Interdisciplinary, Thematic Approach by T. Roger Taylor (#297093)

Dimensions of Learning by Robert J. Marzano and Debra Pickering (#295195)

Leading for Learning in the Digital Age (#200185)

Taking the Ho Hum out of Teaching: Strategies for Embedding Thinking Skills in the Curriculum by Robert Hanson and T. Robert Hanson (#200179)

Teachers as Decision Makers: Designing Integrated Curriculum (#299196)

Print Products
Design as a Catalyst for Learning by Meredith Davis, Peter Hawley, Bernard McMullan, and Gertrude Spilka (#197022)

A Different Kind of Classroom: Teaching with Dimensions of Learning by Robert J. Marzano (#61192107)

Dimensions of Learning Teacher's Manual, 2nd Edition, by Robert J. Marzano, Debra Pickering, and others (#197133)

Dimensions of Learning Trainer's Manual, 2nd Edition, by Robert J. Marzano, Debra Pickering, and others (#197134)

A New Vision for Staff Development by Dennis Sparks and Stephanie Hirsh (#197018)

Videotapes
Dimensions of Learning Videotape Package (6 tapes) (#614236)

How to Engage Students in Critical Thinking Skills ("How To" Series, Tape 8) (#400050)

For more information, visit us on the World Wide Web (http://www.ascd.org), send an e-mail message to member@ascd.org, call the ASCD Service Center (1-800-933-ASCD or 703-578-9600, then press 2), send a fax to 703-575-5400, or write to Information Services, ASCD, 1703 N. Beauregard St., Alexandria, VA 22311-1714 USA.